W9-AVS-590

GRADUATE

FROM COLLEGE

DEBT-FREE

GRADUATE

FROM COLLEGE

DEBT-FREE

Get Your Degree With
Money In The Bank!

BART ASTOR

Humanix Books
www.humanixbooks.com

Humanix Books

Graduate College Debt Free
Copyright © 2016 by Humanix Books
All rights reserved

Humanix Books, P.O. Box 20989, West Palm Beach, FL 33416, USA
www.humanixbooks.com | info@humanixbooks.com

Library of Congress Cataloging-in-Publication Data

Names: Astor, Bart, author.
Title: Graduate college debt-free : get your degree with money in the bank / Bart Astor.
Description: West Palm Beach, FL : Humanix Books, [2016] | Includes index.
Identifiers: LCCN 2016019518| ISBN 9781630060688 (pbk.) | ISBN 9781630060695
    (E-book)
Subjects: LCSH: Student aid—United States—Handbooks, manuals, etc. |
    Student loans—United States—Handbooks, manuals, etc. | College costs—
    United States—Handbooks, manuals, etc.
Classification: LCC LB2337.4 .A85 2016 | DDC 378.30973—dc23
LC record available at https://lccn.loc.gov/2016019518

No part of this book may be reproduced or transmitted in any form or by any means, electronic or mechanical, including photocopying, recording, or by any other information storage and retrieval system, without written permission from the publisher.

Cover Photo: © Image Source / Alamy Stock Photo, Image ID B8DR6W
Cover Design: Tom Lau
Interior Design: Scribe, Inc.

Humanix Books is a division of Humanix Publishing, LLC. Its trademark, consisting of the words "Humanix" is registered in the Patent and Trademark Office and in other countries.

Disclaimer: The information in this book is intended solely for information purposes and is not to be construed, under any circumstances, by implication or otherwise, as an offer to sell or a solicitation to buy or sell or trade in any commodities, currencies, or securities herein named. Information is obtained from sources believed to be reliable, but is in no way guaranteed. No guarantee of any kind is implied or possible where projections of future conditions are attempted. Past results are no indication of future performance. All investments are subject to risk, which should be considered prior to making any investment decisions. Consult your personal investment advisers before making an investment decision.

The information presented in this book is meant to be used for general resource purposes only; it is not intended as specific financial advice for any individual and should not substitute financial advice from a finance professional.

CSS/Financial Aid PROFILE® is a trademark registered by the College Board, which was not involved in the production of, and does not endorse, this product.

ISBN: 978–1-63006–068–8 (Trade Paper)
ISBN: 978–1-63006–069–5 (E-book)

Printed in the United States of America
10 9 8 7 6 5 4 3 2 1

Contents

To Ethan, Jordyn, Zoë, and Ian:
our hope for the future.

Acknowledgments

Helping students pay for college has been a concept in this country for more than four hundred years, but it became a priority first in the mid-1800s when state colleges were established to help keep costs low for residents, then with the GI Bill in the 1940s that enabled millions of returning soldiers to attend college, and then with the passage of the 1965 Higher Education Act that created the system we have now. The architects of that law and later reauthorizations need to be thanked for their incredible contribution to equal opportunity and a more mobile society: former president Lyndon Johnson; senators Wayne Morse, Claiborne Pell, William Stafford, Paul Simon, Walter Mondale, Winston Prouty, and Ted Kennedy; representatives Edith Green, William Ford, and Patsy Mink; Secretary of Health, Education, and Welfare John Gardner, Commissioner of Education Francis Keppel, and a host of visionaries who established the foundation of our current system of need-based financial aid.

On a more personal level, I thank my wife, Kathie Little-Astor, not only for her support in writing this book, but also for being my first tutor and ongoing expert in financial aid. It was she who taught me the concepts of access, choice, and persistence that lay at the heart of financial aid.

I thank my good friend of many years and editor, Debra Englander, who brought me into this project and supported my strong beliefs.

I thank the management and staff of Humanix Books for welcoming me into their family.

I thank the publisher, Mary Glenn; the director of publishing, Sherrie Slopianka; and the cover designer, Tom Lau. I thank David Levy and Mark Kantrowitz for writing their book, *Filing the FAFSA*, a helpful guide to me and thousands of students; The College Board for allowing me to use the screen prints of the CSS PROFILE (especially Susan McCrackin for paving the way); and the many dedicated financial aid colleagues from whom I've learned so much. These are the folks who helped me serve the greater good and who now continue the good fight for students. Please don't stop now—there is still so much to do.

Foreword

Kerry Hannon

When I reflect on the core gifts in my life, education rises to the top. My Irish grandmother frequently reminded me as a child that "no one can take from you what you have between your ears."

I knew what she meant—even as a child—that I *owned* my knowledge, and it was my tool to use to live a successful life both personally and professionally.

I was lucky to have parents who believed in the power of education. My father did not have the financial bandwidth to go to college. He was a child of the Depression, and he had to start working to support himself from an early age.

Dad was ambitious, successful, and determined to provide his four children with the education he himself had had to cobble together on his own. He invested in us, in our education.

Dad's thirst for knowledge was palpable. Even into his eighties he was attending lectures on robotics at Carnegie Mellon University and reading voraciously.

His investment in our education paid dividends—far beyond his joy of visiting us on campus and attending our graduations. I have clung to the energy and possibility that come from learning, which he demonstrated on a daily basis. I, too, am driven to continually learn new things and channel my grandmother's and father's inner curiosity about the world.

Education has made my life a rich one—far beyond the monetary definition of that word.

Today, a college education is, in many ways, nonnegotiable. As I survey the job market as a career expert and travel the country giving speeches to jobseekers of all ages, it's irrefutable that employers value a college education and beyond more than ever.

CareerBuilder, for example, recently put out a survey of more than 2,300 hiring and human resource managers that found that nearly a third of employers have increased their educational requirements over the past five years.

More than a quarter are hiring employees with master's degrees for positions primarily held by those with four-year degrees in the past, and 37 percent are hiring employees with college degrees for positions that had been primarily held by those with high school degrees.

When asked why they are hiring more employees with college degrees for positions that had been primarily for those with high school diplomas in the past, 60 percent of these employers said skills for those positions have evolved, requiring higher-educated labor.

As a result of increasing their educational requirements, employers have witnessed a positive impact on higher-quality work, productivity, communication, innovation/idea generation, and yep, revenue.

Higher degrees not only boost candidates' chances of being hired, but they can help their chances of getting promoted as well—more than a third of employers say they are unlikely to promote someone who doesn't have a college degree.

One of *my* go-to experts in the field of education and life transitions is Bart Astor.

I've found Astor's advice to be down-to-earth, direct, and achievable. It ranges from big-picture considerations to seemingly modest moves someone can make to finance and find true value in higher education.

I wholeheartedly agree with Astor that education is valuable not only in higher wages you'll get throughout your life but in many other ways that he details, including future prospects for your family, security, community involvement, and even better health.

In college, there are things you soak up in the classroom and glean from wise professors, but it's what you learn around campus that magnifies the college experience and this chapter of your life. It's a combination of nurturing relationships and dealing with life on your own that lays the groundwork for navigating the uncertain and unpredictable trail ahead and building a successful future.

In his superb and informative book *Graduate from College Debt-Free*, Astor has woven his succinct advice together to offer optimism and expert guidance for young adults and their parents on the cusp of embarking on a college degree.

Astor's book pulls apart the financial aid process to help you find ways to minimize your out-of-pocket costs using various methods. But his underlying theme is—education is worth it.

Bingo. Whether you are eighteen or eighty, education is the root of finding meaning and joy in the work you do every day. It allows you to make a positive impact on the world.

Yes, college generally has a tangible payoff. Overall, those with four-year college degrees make more money, period.

Even more important than the financial rewards, investing in education is imperative in today's rapidly changing workplace, particularly if you gain skills in, say, finance or marketing that are transportable to other industries as your career evolves over the decades.

That said, I would be remiss to ignore the genuine fears I have for twenty-somethings graduating with weighty debt burdens. "Debt is a *dream killer*" is one of *my* refrains. It limits your choices about the kinds of careers you can pursue and jobs you can accept. When you're trapped by the need for a certain size of paycheck to pay the bills and whittle down debt, you lose your freedom to pursue your passions.

In 1989, only 17 percent of those in their twenties and early thirties had student debt; today, 42 percent do, according to the Federal Reserve Survey of Consumer Finances.

And that's troublesome. Of those who financed college through loans, the class of 2015 was saddled with $35,000 in debt on average, with monthly payments of about $380 on average. Astor is here to help you face that challenge squarely.

Graduate from College Debt-Free is your manual to a healthier, more prosperous life. Read this book for the encouragement, advice, and tools to help you uncover smart ways to take the reins of your education and jump start your career.

Kerry Hannon, author of *Great Jobs for Everyone 50+* and *Love Your Job: The New Rules for Career Happiness*

Introduction

Let me make something very clear right from the start: I'm a charter member of the college attendance fan club. I think just about everyone will benefit from going to college. And, moreover, I think everyone should have an opportunity to attend! But that's not just my own personal opinion; by almost every measure, this viewpoint is backed up by facts.

1. *Income.* While I don't think how much money you can make is a very reliable measure of success, the facts are abundantly clear: college graduates earn more over their lifetime than non–college grads. Even by attending a year or two, regardless of which college you go to, you will make more money than if you don't attend at all. Of course, there are certainly exceptions. But if you're one of those exceptional people, this book is probably not for you. You're already exceptional, and chances are there's not too much I can tell you that you don't already know.

2. *Quality of life.* A college education will improve the quality of your life in so many ways, it's hard

to enumerate them all. Here are a few important considerations:

   a. As they get older, earnings of college grads rise more rapidly.
   b. Unemployment rates are significantly lower for college grads than for non–college grads.
   c. Significantly fewer college grads live in households that rely on income-supporting government programs (e.g., SNAP and National School Lunch Program).
   d. College-educated adults are more likely to receive health insurance and retirement benefits from employers.
   e. College-educated adults are less likely to be obese, and children who live in households with more-educated parents are less likely to be obese.

3. *Citizenship*. People with higher levels of education are more active citizens as adults:

   a. A much higher percentage of those who attended college, even those who attended for just a year or two, volunteer for organizations.
   b. Four-fifths of those who graduated from college voted in the last presidential election, compared with just over half of high school grads.

4. *Parenting and the future*. The future is brighter for children of college-educated parents.

   a. College-educated mothers spend more time with their children than do less-educated mothers, and that's true of mothers who are employed and mothers who are not.
   b. Children of parents who attended college are significantly more likely to go to college than children of parents who did not go to college.

So do you see why I'm so pro-college? The future is brighter when more people have the opportunity to get additional education. Is it all cause and effect? Of course not. There are many other factors that help drive these statistics. But everyone should want to maximize his or her opportunities in life, and going to college helps accomplish that.

🎓 Hey, It's Only Money

With the understanding that I am totally pro-college, and knowing that this book will help you ease the financial hardship of paying for college, don't be too surprised on occasion to read "Hey, it's only money."

What do I mean? Simply put, when you're making financial decisions, they often deal with a few thousand dollars that wind up being paid out over the course of your lifetime. Or at least, we can reasonably say over many years. That's particularly true when it comes to loans. I don't have too much concern about a decision that costs you $5,000 or $10,000, a sum that is spread over a ten-year period after you get a college degree.

That said, I am acutely aware of how $5,000—or even $500—can be a make-or-break situation for many of you readers. Among my jobs, I worked as the director of financial aid at a community college in California. Whether a student had $50 to $100 available was a big deal and often meant the difference between eating and not eating that day and the next. That's why we established short-term emergency cash funds to help students with these immediate concerns.

So I'm not talking about daily expenses of living. Cash flow is difficult to manage, and we will focus on it later in this book. When I say "Hey, it's only money," I mean the bigger picture. I'm talking about the decision about which college to attend, whether to take a loan, and what to major in. We know that engineers generally can make more money than humanities grads. But should you choose to major in one of the STEM fields when you have no interest or aptitude in science? What have you accomplished? Of course, having taken math and science courses will help you in whatever field you pursue. But by majoring in a field of study that's not right for you, you risk entering a field that makes you unhappy. If making a lot of money is your goal, then sure, go for it. Take the courses that will get you to your goal. But I suspect that most of you who are reading this are looking at college (either for yourself or for your child) not only as a moneymaker but as the best way to get better prepared for life.

CHAPTER 1

How Much *Does* It Cost?

🎓 Cost and Choice

The first thing most of you want to know about a college is "How much will it cost to send my child there?" That, you figure, will guide your child's choice of which college to attend. Not necessarily. And I hope in my opening remarks you realized that cost is only one of many factors to consider.

Here's my mantra:

The cost of a college should not determine which college you or your child attends.

That's easy enough to say, but for the most part, it's true. First of all, until you do your analysis and until you know what kind of financial aid you'll be awarded, you really don't know what the cost will be. The sticker price of a college, much like the sticker price of a car, is not typically what you and the student will pay. Too many parents tell their children from an early age that the only place they can go is the local community college or the state college because the parents think that is the only place they can afford.

But the fact is, very few families pay the sticker price, and sometimes the college or university that looks to be the most expensive turns out to require the least amount of money from you. That's where financial aid comes into play. It's also about the commitment that the college itself makes to the student, some of which translates into discounting the out-of-pocket costs.

Net Price Calculators

First, you should always check the college's website for what is called the "net price" of the college. Every college, by law, must provide or refer potential students to a net price calculator. That's a tool students can use to determine the actual out-of-pocket costs to the family. It's the sticker price minus the amount of grants and scholarships awarded. The figures provided are based on averages from the college and often the information the student provides about family income and academics. Frankly, it's really the only legitimate method of comparing college costs. But keep in mind that these calculators are only helpful estimates, not actual numbers. The tool cannot predict how much merit scholarship money a student will receive. It can only estimate how much need-based grant and scholarship money the student will be awarded.

Still, while it's not 100 percent accurate, it is a key tool that you definitely want to use before making your decisions. And you should consider using a net price calculator before you eliminate any college you have been considering.

Now let's look more deeply into the actual costs.

Common Educational Charges

There are several categories of expenses that usually make up the total cost of education at any college:

- tuition and fees
- room and board
- travel and transportation
- books and supplies
- personal and miscellaneous expenses

Tuition and Fees

Tuition and fees are the amounts colleges charge students to attend. For most traditional colleges, this category is a flat amount based on full-time enrollment as defined by the college. And full-time generally means taking enough credits (or units as some call them) to graduate in four years. Some colleges divide the years in half and refer to each half as a semester; some use the quarter system, requiring three or four per year. To graduate in four years having accumulated 120 credits, a typical requirement, a student would have to take at least 30 credits per year. A full-time course load would then equal 15 credits per semester. Naturally there are some other restrictions having to do with specific course requirements in your major and some general education requirements. But overall, students can usually graduate in four years or less by going full-time for the four years (some students can accelerate their studies by taking summer courses or taking a larger number of credits per semester).

Tuition varies greatly among colleges and universities. Public colleges are partially supported by state tax dollars, so the tuition at public institutions is considerably less for in-state residents. Many students who attend a public college in a different state try to establish residency in order to pay the lower tuition. But states have very specific requirements, and most students find it difficult to establish themselves as state residents while in college.

Students who attend part-time generally pay a proportionate amount.

Fees are school-specific and vary enormously. They usually have a specific purpose, such as student activities and health services. But in some states, the fee is just another term for the tuition. When colleges refer to fees, they generally mean that all students are required to pay them, as opposed to something like a lab breakage fee, which only students taking a lab course must pay.

So most of the time, tuition and fees are lumped together and the amounts are listed on the college website and promotional materials.

Options for Lowering Costs of Tuition and Fees

- Attend part-time. But keep in mind that this strategy will require you attend for more years so there may not be any savings. Also note that part-time students don't succeed as often as full-timers.
- Finish early by taking more than a full-time load. Taking more credits often does not cost more than the full-time load. But be careful that you don't take on more academic work than you can handle.
- Take classes during the summers. But keep in mind that going to school in the summer means that you can't work during the summer when you could otherwise be earning money for college.
- Attend an in-state public college. The tuition will be less, but as I said earlier, your out-of-pocket costs may not be any lower because of financial aid. Plus, the public college may not be one of the student's prime choices, so he or she may not have as positive an experience as he or she would at a school more appropriate to the student's needs. And most state colleges are large, so students may

Table 1.1: Cost of Education (2015–16)

Tuition and fees	Public two-year	Public four-year (in-state)	Public four-year (out-of-state)	Private nonprofit four-year (on-campus)
Tuition/fees	$3,435	$9,410	$23,893	$32,405
Room/board	$8,003	$10,138	$10,138	$11,516
Books/supplies	$1,364	$1,298	$1,298	$1,249
Transportation	$1,774	$1,109	$1,109	$1,033
Other expenses	$2,257	$2,106	$2,106	$1,628
Total	$16,833	$24,061	$38,544	$47,831

Source: The College Board, Annual Survey of Colleges.

not always be able to get the classes they want (in order to graduate in four years).

- Attend a lower-cost, two-year community college. Again, although the tuition will be less, your out-of-pocket costs may not be any lower because of financial aid (and most community colleges have very little discretionary financial aid).

Room and Board

The second-highest expense at most colleges is the amount a student must pay for room and board, which includes housing and meals. Whether it's living on campus in a dorm or off campus in private housing, a significant part of a student's budget is the living expenses. Fortunately, it's also the category over which you have the most control. The dorm rates are generally pretty much set, but there are often cheaper alternatives, not the least of which is for the student to live at home. Although there are still costs associated with that option, it's something you're already used to, and it may not impact your budget since the housing portion doesn't change when the student leaves or stays.

Options for Lowering Costs of Living Expenses

- Live at home. Your mortgage/rent payment will remain the same, so you won't have the additional housing expenses, and the cost of food will not change from what you've already been paying. But the student does lose the experience of going away to college, a valuable lesson in life. And don't forget the cost of commuting, especially by car. On campus, students rarely, if ever, have cars.
- Share an apartment. Sometimes dorms can be more expensive than private housing, especially if the student shares a small apartment. But again, don't forget to add in the cost of commuting. And this option is not always the best for students who want a campus experience. Plus, students don't always have the easiest time budgeting for food and consequently may end up spending more by ordering in food or going out to eat.
- Work as a resident advisor. These positions are for those who are in their upper class years or for graduate students and come with free room and board (generally in lieu of a salary).
- Work in food services. Sometimes, if a student works in a food establishment, either on or off campus, the student will have access to meals, thus saving on a meal plan or buying his or her own food.

Living Away from Home: Leaving high school and going college is one of the rites of passage that mark a transition from childhood to adulthood. There are many social and developmental advantages to living away from home while attending college, even if the college is within commuting distance.

Travel and Transportation

Another relatively large expense for most students is the cost of getting to and from the college, whether the student is commuting daily or simply getting to the college and back home during breaks. This expense is quite variable and depends on the distance from home, mode of transportation, and the frequency of the student's visits back home. In determining budgets, most colleges assume that the student will return home two or three times during the year. For commuters, the budget will likely be equivalent to bus or public transportation costs, although some colleges will allow for reasonable car expenses.

Because this is such a variable expense, if the estimate provided by the college is not accurate, you can easily appeal this, as long as you have reasonable documentation and a good reason for any additional expense (i.e., a college will not include the finance expenses of leasing or buying a car, just the cost of driving to and from the college).

Options for Lowering Costs of Travel/Transportation

- Buy airplane tickets early to save on fares, subscribe to a service such as Hopper that tracks fares, or use frequent flyer miles.
- Use public transportation when possible since the cost of operating a car is generally a lot higher.
- Carpool to campus if living off campus.
- Drive to and from home with a buddy.

Books and Supplies

Although the cost of books and supplies is a lot higher than you might expect, it's still a fraction of the total cost. Schools and individual programs within colleges will have varying costs for books and supplies (art supplies will cost more, for example), but the total cost for books is somewhere between $2,000 and $2,500 per year. That's a lot of money, but again, it's a small percentage of the total cost.

Options for Lowering Costs of Books and Supplies

- Look to buy used books. They typically sell out quickly, but if you plan far enough in advance, you may be able to find at least some of the required books. But don't wait too long to buy, otherwise even the new books may not be available.
- Use an older model of computer with less memory instead of buying the very latest model with all the bells and whistles. Rarely will schoolwork require the kind of memory needed for gaming.
- Consider purchasing a refurbished computer. Just make sure there is a warranty and that it has all the software you'll need.
- See if you can use a campus computer rather than buying a new one.

Personal and Miscellaneous Expenses

Part of every budget for school costs is the category of personal expenses. This covers all the individual things you have to buy to live, and not just at the bare minimum. This includes a modest amount for recreation, personal hygiene, laundry, and so on. If you have any special needs—for example, you require special medicine—then the cost should be included here. And be sure to let the financial aid office know so that these necessities can be counted in the budget the aid officials calculate for you.

Options for Lowering Personal and Miscellaneous Expenses

- Be frugal. You don't have to live just on ramen, but eating out and drinking a lot will take a huge toll on your budget. So cut down on personal expenses wherever you can, but not so much that you get sick or that college becomes a negative experience for you.

- Take advantage of the fact that families can buy health insurance for their children up to the age of twenty-six. Colleges will offer health insurance to students, but the premium is likely to be much higher than what you can get through your parents.
- Be careful about blowing your budget. Extra expenses for cars are generally not included in budgets for students who live on campus. And certainly there will be no allowance for questionable expenses like parking tickets, library fines, and lab breakage.
- Switch to a reasonable data plan and/or participate in a family plan that has lower monthly charges. High-cost data plans are not encouraged in your college budget. Be vigilant about not going over your limit, either in texts or minutes. And whenever possible—most likely everywhere on campus—be logged into Wi-Fi so you can use Internet communication rather than cellular.

Access and Choice

I said at the beginning of this chapter that, ideally, the cost of a college should not determine which college you or your child attends. I believe strongly that money should not be the determining factor. But with private colleges costing more than a quarter of a million dollars, money is inevitably a factor. In the past, financial aid at least partially succeeded in leveling the playing field between public and private colleges. This is still somewhat true, but it's not quite as easy to see right away. Although net price calculators help students know early on what their out-of-pocket costs will be, they are only estimates, and you won't really know until your final financial aid award is received. Still, that's a big help, and you should not rule out any college based on money until you've used the college's own or one of the other net price calculators available. You could see right away that the supposedly lower-cost public university might actually cost you more than the expensive private institution. Or not.

Financial Aid: The purpose of financial aid is to make it possible for students to attend the college that best fits their academic abilities and goals regardless of how much it costs.

That said, my final bits of advice for this chapter—before we get into the specifics about financial aid—are these:

1. Do not rule out any college you are interested in until you crunch the numbers using a net price calculator.
2. Do not rule out any college you are interested in until you receive the final financial aid award letters from the colleges you apply to.

Now let's start talking about paying for all these costs.

CHAPTER 2

Paying for College

A Shared Responsibility

A college education will be the foundation for a lifetime of learning and personal growth, well beyond graduation. Make sure you're making a sound investment.

Michael Steidel, dean of admission,
Carnegie Mellon University

A Huge Investment

The sticker price for four years at the high-end private colleges is now more than $250,000 when you add in all the costs. That's serious money. Even the total four-year cost at a public college is well over $100,000.

My question to you is, If you were considering purchasing a sizeable investment like a house, would you even for a moment consider paying for the whole purchase in four years? Of course not. Whether you're buying a house that costs $250,000 or one for $100,000, chances are you would save up enough money to make a down payment and then you would get a mortgage for the rest of the purchase price that would allow you to pay for the house over an extended period, often 30 years.

Why wouldn't you view paying for college in a similar way? The investment you make in yourself (or in your child) by going to college is one I have already enumerated; the return on investment is whopping and the nonfinancial return equally significant. Suppose you thought of college in this same way. Here's the scenario:

Child's early years: you'd begin saving for the down payment. Fortunately, there are some excellent ways to do so that allow the savings to grow tax-free and also permit you to deduct the amount you save in special accounts from your income tax liability.

Child approaching college: you'd investigate which college is the right college for your child and which will accept him or her. Then you'd calculate the out-of-pocket costs (by subtracting grants and scholarships offered), determine how much you and the student can afford to pay from your total current income, plan how much the student can earn while in college and during breaks to help pay, learn about ways to defer the remaining amount of the purchase through loans, and choose the appropriate loan type and amount based on your calculations and the terms of the extended payments are.

Child graduates from college: you and your child start paying back what was loaned to you. You set up a repayment plan that's appropriate for you from among several options (including income-based plans); you refinance the loans if you find better terms; you consolidate the loans if you can and if that option gives you better payment terms; your child defers payments if he or she goes back to get an advanced degree; you stay in touch with the lender so as to not ruin your credit rating; you apply for any loan forgiveness available through employers and government programs; you apply for forbearance if you lose your job or if payments become too burdensome; you do everything you can to avoid defaulting on your loans; and you smile knowing that the purchase you made of a college education, regardless of whether you paid more than you could have, can never be repossessed.

That's the scenario you need to keep in mind. And let me say this once again: your college education can never be repossessed.

🎓 Paying for College

The first time your child's eyes open and see your beaming smile may not be the time you think about your baby's college education, but hopefully those thoughts will follow not too much later. As the old saying goes, "The best time to start saving for your children's education is the day they're born. The second best time is today."

If your child is already older than a few months and you haven't started saving for his or her college education, don't wait. There's still a lot you can do to help pay. And, more important, there's a lot you can do to help give your child choices and opportunities.

The Before Years: What You Can Do Before College to Help Save Money

   i. Savings

      a. Traditional Savings/Investments: Obviously one of the easiest ways to begin saving for your or your child's education is to start putting money into a savings account. The beauty of this is the simplicity and flexibility of these kinds of accounts, which include money market accounts, savings accounts, or even certificates of deposit. But of course, that flexibility also means that these accounts can easily be used for other purposes, robbing your child of the funds you had ostensibly saved for him or her. There are a myriad of ways to save and invest in traditional accounts, but I would emphasize that since doing so is not specific for your child's education, this method is not the most reliable. Still, it is better than nothing, and if you often find yourself living hand to mouth, having this money as a backup can help you through those tough times. Just be sure to replenish any funds you use for noneducational purposes.

b. 529 Savings Plans: These savings plans, so called because that is the specific section in the IRS code, are vehicles families can use to save for educational expenses. The beauty of these plans is that the earnings from the plan are not subject to taxes if the money is used to pay for college expenses. In addition, the money you put into the plan may be tax deductible for state taxes (though not for federal taxes). You can open a plan administered by any state or institution (and often other states have plans that have better yields or lower costs), but you can only deduct your contributions from your state taxes if you live in the state where you open the 529 plan. There are limits to the amount you can contribute annually (currently anything more than $14,000 per individual contribution to one beneficiary is the limit) and there are other restrictions about the use of the plan. However, the plans have some flexibility; if the designated beneficiary does not use the funds, the money can be used by someone else, as long as the funds are used to pay for educational expenses.

c. 529 Prepaid Tuition Plans: These plans, similar to 529 savings plans, are state-specific and, as the name implies, the funds are only good at colleges in the state. The value and increase follow totally different rules from 529 savings plans. Whereas 529 plans increase or decrease in value just like any other investment, prepaid tuition plans increase at the same rate as college tuition. It's like locking in the tuition at the current rate. If the tuition doubles, the plan value also doubles. So if you prepaid the entire year's tuition and your child is five or ten years away from attending, when the tuition will likely increase, the amount you have will still be enough to pay for that one year. That's a great benefit because it takes out a lot of the uncertainty. However, it also requires that your child attend a college in the state. For more information about all the 529 plans, check with your financial adviser or click here (https://www.irs.gov/pub/irs-pdf/p970.pdf).

2. College Credit for Previous Coursework or "Life Experience"

   a. Advanced Placement (AP) Classes: At some colleges, AP classes taken in high school can count toward a four-year degree, thus reducing the number of credits required to graduate. At many colleges, however, AP classes do not reduce the number required in college but are used as admission criteria and allow students to skip the basic introductory courses. The elite, highly selective colleges, for example, almost require high school students to take as many AP classes as possible and do not reduce the number required in college. At other colleges, students have to score at least a four or five out of five on the AP test to qualify for college credit. When considering AP classes as a way to reduce your expenses, check with the colleges themselves. Also keep in mind that taking these beginning classes while in high school allows bright students to take even more advanced courses when they get to college, and the purpose of college is not simply to qualify for graduation but to learn as much as you can.

b. Dual Enrollment: Many colleges offer qualifying students the opportunity to take college-level classes at the college while still enrolled in high school and allow the student to get credit at both schools. Dual enrollment allows students to get a leg up on the number of credits they need to graduate.

c. Life Experience: Some colleges will allow students who have some experience beyond high school to use that experience as an equivalent to college credit, thereby reducing the number of credits students must pay for. While this mostly applies to older students who, indeed, have had some "life experience," it can also be appropriate for some young people who have had summer or high school internships. Typically, though, the colleges that offer life experience credit are online colleges or distance-learning programs offered by many traditional universities, and the kind of experience is often related to training while on the job or having gained a certificate of proficiency or a license in a specific field.

d. College Level Exam Program (CLEP) and DAN-TES Subject Standardized Tests (DSST): Generally for older students who have been out of school for a while, these programs allow students to take an exam to prove proficiency in the equivalent of freshman year coursework. Many online and some traditional colleges will allow students up to thirty credits earned by passing the exam. This is equal to about one full year of college work. For more information, again refer to the college; The College Board (https://www.collegeboard.org), which administers the CLEP program; and Get College Credit (http://getcollegecredit.com), which administers the DSST program.

3. Employee Benefits: Many companies offer tuition benefits to their employees, and some extend that benefit to the dependents of employees. This can lead to substantial savings, so it is definitely something you should check on by speaking with your Human Resources department.

4. Veterans Benefits: Administered by the US Department of Veterans Affairs, the GI Bill provides both tuition and living expense benefits to veterans. If you, your spouse, or your parent is a veteran, you should check with the Veterans Administration (http://www.benefits.va.gov/gibill) before making decisions about which college to attend.

5. Scholarship Search: Heard the one about the "millions of dollars in scholarship money [that] goes unclaimed?" Although there are, indeed, some scholarships that are never awarded, that advertising teaser is mostly false. Included in the claim are potential awards with very restrictive criteria (e.g., the student must be from a particular town, be attending a specific college, and be majoring in a specific field) and, making up a large portion of the claim, employee benefits that are available to employees, but no employee goes to college.

That said, there are, in fact, millions of dollars in private and foundation scholarships that do get awarded, and families should most definitely try to get in on that money. Fortunately, you don't have to do very much to research them. There are free scholarship search engines that allow you to input your data and receive reports that list the available scholarships. But applying for the scholarships themselves will often take a great deal of time and energy. And for the large, significant awards, the competition is very rigorous. Keep in mind, too, that if the student qualifies for need-based financial aid, the scholarship combined with other financial aid awarded cannot be more than the approved budget.

a. Still, applying for scholarships is definitely an important strategy to use in your attempt to graduate debt-free (or almost). Here are some of the free scholarship search websites:

    http://www.fastweb.com

    https://bigfuture.collegeboard.org/scholarship
    -search

    https://www.scholarships.com

    http://www.studentscholarshipsearch.com

    From the US Department of Labor, see

    http://careerinfonet.org/scholarshipsearch/
        ScholarshipCategory.asp?searchtype=
        category&nodeid=22

The Enrolled Years: What You Can Do While in College to Help Save Money

Part of your family's planning before your child enrolls in college is about how you will manage your finances during the college years. Cash flow will very likely be a problem both for the family and for the student. But that's generally manageable as long as the family is not already overburdened. Life inevitably brings surprises, so having as much knowledge as possible of all the costs is critical to success. Colleges will supply detailed budgets, but there are always unforeseen expenses—a car breakdown or an extra trip home, for example—that can throw a wrench in the works. Not only do you need to keep track of all the known expenses, you have to build into your budget a little padding for stuff you haven't considered. And you should also have an emergency payment method, such as a home equity line of credit or separate bank account.

But while the student is enrolled, there are only a handful of sources from which you'll pay for all the college expenses.

1. Savings: This is why you spent all those years stashing away all that money. This is the rainy day. It's the time to tap into the 529 plan that you created those many years ago. There's no reason to hold back now—unless, of course, there are other students still in the home for whom you are also saving. As we delve deeper into the financial aid process, we'll discuss the family contribution (FC) that will be "expected" from you. This is money that the student will not be awarded by the college, money that will be used to pay for the balance of the student's expenses not covered by financial aid, whether they are direct costs paid to the college, like tuition and fees, or indirect costs, like books and supplies or transportation. You can estimate your FC by using one of the family contribution calculators available online (https://bigfuture.collegeboard.org/pay-for-college/ paying-your-share/expected-family-contribution -calculator). Note that there are actually two different calculations you will have to do: one for Federal funds and a second that many colleges use to award their own money. We will discuss this in greater detail when we go over the financial aid process.

2. Current Income: Some of what you'll pay for the student's college expenses will come out of your current income. Acknowledging that most families are already strapped, there is not likely to be a bunch of extra money in the monthly budget. But take solace in knowing that there might actually be a little savings in your home budget, especially if the student is away. If nothing else, the refrigerator won't be empty all the time! But, more than likely, you will find that you need to dig into your savings and other resources to meet the student's expenses. And if there are any assets you have been thinking of selling, this might be a good time to do so, but bear in mind that there may be tax consequences.

3. Student Income: The days of "working your way through college" are long gone. With costs at their current levels and student salaries generally close to minimum wage, it's not likely students will be able to contribute too much during the school year. Consider that $10 per hour for twenty hours per week (a very full workload) yields only $800 per month minus some taxes (FICA), or somewhere in the vicinity of $7,000 per academic year. Although that's a pretty big chunk, it's not going to cover the costs of a year in college, even at a public college. And twenty hours a week is a huge burden on most students. For some it's manageable; for others it could lead to academic disaster. If you're the student, make sure you have realistic expectations about how many hours you can work during the school year. You, as the parent of a student, should also be mindful of the difficulty of juggling work and school.

   a. For summer and school-year breaks, that's a different conversation. For the three or so months of summer break, most students find employment that helps them (and you) pay for the rest of the school year. However, many students also use that time to work for no pay at internships and not-for-profit organizations for which they get little or no monetary reward but great experience that can help them land a good job later on. You and your child need to be clear about what you expect in terms of his or her financial contribution from summertime jobs.

4. Gifts: Although for most families this is a minor category in financing options, the fact is that many grandparents do contribute to the college costs of their grandchildren. If nothing else, they may supply clothing and supplies required for classes. Some grandparents, aunts, and uncles also contribute to the child's 529 plan, which has both positive and negative consequences for the student. We'll talk more about this in our discussion of how financial aid works. But any gift, large or small, will be a welcome addition to the family's financing of the student's education. Of course, the amount anyone can gift another person is taxable when the annual amount is greater than $14,000, either in cash or in kind. But that doesn't preclude two grandparents from gifting $14,000 each without the family incurring a gift tax. Although this is certainly pretty rare, it does happen. And we should point out that when applying for financial aid, applicants must report gifts received directly.

5. Tax Benefits: What do tax benefits have to do with paying for college during the college years? Simple. Lower taxes means more take-home pay if you plan for it by increasing the number of deductions you take. Or it means a larger refund after you file your

taxes. Either way, taking advantage of state and federal tax benefits will net you additional income for the year that you can throw into the college cost pot. Let me be perfectly clear that this is not tax advice. You should check with your tax advisor and/or the Internal Revenue Service (IRS; https://www.irs .gov/uac/Tax-Benefits-for-Education:-Information -Center) about any potential benefit. But, in summary, there are a few strategies to keep in mind.

a. The first strategy is using educational tax credits. There are two types of tax credits: the American Opportunity Tax Credit (up to a maximum of $2,500 per year, per eligible student for up to four years) and the Lifetime Learning Credit (up to a maximum of $2,000 per year, with no limit to the number of years). There are other terms you need to know, so refer to the IRS or your tax advisor.

b. The second strategy is using educational tax deductions. You may be able to deduct education expenses paid for yourself, your spouse, or your children, reducing your taxable income by up to $4,000. Again, consult your tax advisor for more information.

c. You cannot take both an educational tax credit and a deduction so you should choose the one that is better for you.

6. Student Financial Aid: This is undoubtedly the gorilla in the room. About two-thirds of students at four-year public colleges receive financial aid, and that percentage is greater at private colleges. The funds typically come from a variety of sources including the federal government, your state government, the college itself, and private companies or foundations. Most students receive aid in three

forms: grants or scholarships (money you do not have to pay back), work-study (money you earn), and loans (money you have to pay back, generally after you finish college). In the next chapters, we will delve further into the topics of financial aid, the application process, and your responsibilities when receiving aid and repaying loans.

7. Parent Financial Aid: In addition to student financial aid, there are also programs available to the parents of students. Again, there are a variety of sources including the federal government, state government, the college itself, employers, and private lenders such as banks and credit unions. Except for employee benefits, financial assistance to parents is only supplied in the form of loans that have to be paid back either while the student is still in college or after he or she finishes. In later chapters, we will discuss the federal PLUS Loan program in greater detail.

8. Home Equity Lines of Credit (HELOC) and Home Equity Loans: These loans are from private lenders such as banks and credit unions. Homeowners have access to a defined amount based on the homeowner's credit rating and the value of the home itself. For many people, the value of their home—even after the housing bubble—is their single most valuable asset. And if there is equity there—that is, if the home is worth more than what you owe on your mortgage—it may make sense to borrow against that equity to pay for your child's college education. A line of credit means that you can borrow money as you need it, not all at once, which is what a home equity loan requires. That's why, for most people, it's smarter to open a line of credit and only have to pay interest on the amount you need to borrow each year or semester.

a. There are positives and negatives about home equity loans and lines of credit. One positive is, of course, that once you qualify, you have easy access to cash you need, and the payment terms are often quite attractive. Also, the interest rates are generally low, and for many HELOCs, the payments can be stretched out over a long period so as to make them affordable. But you can also pay off the loan as early as you want to. If you receive a bonus or if you find you have a little extra money at the end of the month, for example, you can lower the principal, which effectively lowers the interest rate and the total amount of interest you'll be paying. Many HELOCs are also tax deductible since they are, in effect, a second mortgage on your home. But you should check with a tax advisor to determine whether your HELOC is tax deductible.

b. On the negative side, HELOCs put your house at risk. That's a serious consequence that should not be taken lightly. If your income drops, you may have difficulty paying the loan, and the lender could force you to sell or could foreclose on your home. It would probably be unwise for you to borrow against your home if you are already having difficulty making your current house payments.

9. Tuition Payment Plans: Paying some $25,000 or more all at once at the beginning of every semester can be a huge burden for many families, even with careful planning. Therefore, most private colleges offer a tuition payment plan to qualifying families. Essentially this is a short-term loan that allows you to pay the large tuition amount in multiple payments, not all at once. There are generally

some small fees involved. Usually colleges require that monthly payments begin before the semester begins. For cash flow purposes, these plans can be a big help to families, as long as the costs are low and as long as you're confident you'll be able to make the required payments. Not doing so can not only jeopardize your credit rating but also threaten your child's enrollment. And don't forget about the possibility of paying the tuition bill using a credit card that offers cash rebates, frequent flyer miles, or rewards. Some offer as much as a 5 percent rebate. That's a pretty hefty sum that can reduce your out-of-pocket expense significantly.

The After Years: What You Can Do to Save Money After the Student Finishes College

If you think resources to help pay while the student is in college are limited, once the student graduates, there are even fewer options. But indeed, there are some. And ironically, these could provide some of the biggest cost savings overall.

Loans. Presumably you and the student will have taken out loans to help finance his or her education. Hopefully you'll have chosen the loans with the best terms available. We will provide a more thorough review of the loans later in this book. There are many things to consider regarding the terms of the loan, and there are different loans available to parents than there are to students. As a general rule, federally backed student loans are best for students, partially because of the interest rate, but also because of the repayment options. Federal parent loans, on the other hand, do not offer the same kinds of benefits, and it's likely you'll find other loan options elsewhere that have lower interest rates with comparable terms.

When thinking about how to save money on your loan, the interest rate is one of the most important factors. But there are other terms that are important to consider. For student loans, you have the option of deferring any payment for six months after you graduate. (That six-month deferral may not apply if you drop out of school.) That gives you time to find a job and set up an apartment before you have to begin paying. Also, if you have multiple loans from different sources, you might want to be able to consolidate several loans into one larger one. That often reduces the monthly payment because of minimum payment amounts. In addition, some federal loans have deferments available if the student goes back to school at least half-time. Depending on the type of loan, the interest may or may not continue to accrue when you get a deferment, so you'll want to be sure to know once repayment has begun. And one of the most important choices students have to make is the kind of repayment plan. We will explore this more later, but this is where borrowers not only can save the most money but, even more important, can avoid being delinquent or going into default.

For parent loans, there are fewer options and very limited deferment benefits. Home equity loans may be tax deductible, thus saving you money on your taxes. And you should be sure to check with your tax advisor. But for the most part, the driving factor for parent loans will be the interest rate, which may depend on your credit score. So try to have as clean a credit rating as possible; doing so could save you thousands of dollars.

Loan Forgiveness. There are two government-sponsored loan forgiveness programs, Teacher Loan Forgiveness and Public Service Loan Forgiveness.

> *Teacher Loan Forgiveness*: Intended to encourage people to either enter or continue working as teachers, this federal government program offers the opportunity to have some or all of your student loans forgiven. You must work for five consecutive years in a school district that qualifies for Title I funds or has

been selected by the US Department of Education because more than 30 percent of the students qualify for Title I funds. Check here (https://studentaid.ed.gov/sa/repay-loans/forgiveness-cancellation/teacher) for more details about the requirements.

Public Service Loan Forgiveness: If you work full-time for the government or for a not-for-profit organization, regardless of your particular responsibilities, and you make ten years of payments (120 months), the balance of your loan may be forgiven. Check here (https://studentaid.ed.gov/sa/repay-loans/forgiveness-cancellation/public-service) for more details about the program.

Employee Benefit (Recruitment). One of the new and good phenomena that have occurred as a result of the media hype about excessive student debt is the willingness of employers to use loan payment as a recruitment tool. Some are even offering signing bonuses. If you agree to work for such a firm, the employer agrees to pay a specific amount toward your student loans. Each employer's plan is different—that is, some require a year's service or more before they reimburse you for your loan payments; others pay up front, but if you leave the company, you would have to either repay the amount they paid you or have it deducted from your severance or future paychecks. For the most part, these are great deals. But remember that the money an employer pays on your behalf may be taxable, so you may have to pay taxes on it. It also means that you are probably getting a lower salary than if the company didn't have to pay anything toward your student loans. Still, if you are lucky enough to be offered a job at a firm offering this benefit, you can crunch the numbers and determine whether it's the best deal for you.

A Word About Student Loans. As we will stress later, staying current on your student loans will make your life much easier in so many ways. If you fall behind, not only will your credit rating suffer, meaning that you may not be able to buy that new car or even rent an apartment (many landlords are requiring a clean credit rating for renters), but there are other important considerations. For example, many jobs require that you not be in default of a federal loan, and not just government jobs. If you work for a company that does business with the federal government—even if you don't work on that contract—you may be declared ineligible for the job if you are in default of a federal loan. Needless to say, that will impact your ability to repay the loan. Furthermore, the loan forgiveness program and employee recruitment benefit just discussed will likely not be offered if you are already in default. So I'll say it here and again later: *do not go into default on your student loan.* There are options you have to avoid default, and sometimes all you have to do is contact your lender to help you through rough spots.

Work Commitment. A little-used method of lowering your college costs is your commitment to working for an organization for a period of time in exchange for the employer paying for your education. This is a bit different from employee benefits offered from current employers. It's a strategy that was often used many years ago but has been almost nonexistent for quite a while. However, it now seems to be coming back in favor, although it is generally limited to graduate school. Still, it's worth mentioning given the chance that it does grow or that more companies pick it up as an employee recruiting tool. Essentially, you agree to work for a particular organization after you finish college, and in exchange, that organization agrees to pay your college costs or provides you with a stipend while you're enrolled. If you don't work for the organization, you have to pay back the benefit just as if it was a loan. It's rare now, but still something you can explore if there is a particular company with which you have a relationship.

College Access, Choice, and Persistence

At the beginning of this book, I made the statement "Hey, it's only money," adding that when decisions are being made about which college to attend, out-of-pocket costs of around a few thousand dollars are driving the decision. Over the course of your lifetime, that doesn't sound like much, even though at the time, it's a lot of money. But what I hope is that choosing the college that's best for you or your child will mean considering many variables, only one of which is money. I won't go into detail about all the *other* factors you should consider, but here are some:

- availability of the program you are most interested in
- specific professors you want to work with
- ease of getting into the classes you want and need to take
- big school versus small school
- institute versus university
- availability of graduate programs
- academic reputation and rigor
- distance from home
- location (big city, small town, rural, college town, etc.)
- legacy (other family members having attended)
- friends who attend
- the "feel" you have when you visit the campus
- out-of-pocket costs (net price) after considering financial aid, scholarships, and other benefits

Suppose the cost to you was the same at each of the colleges you are considering. Suppose there was a mechanism to make that a reality. That's exactly what financial aid is all about. And while we'll dig more deeply into the specific programs in the next chapter, here's a quick review of how financial aid provides both access to and choice of college you want to attend.

It starts with the underlying principles of student financial aid developed more than sixty years ago, summarized as "access, choice, and persistence."

1. Families have the primary responsibility of paying for college *to the extent they are able.*
2. The purpose of financial aid is to make it possible for students to attend the college that best fits their academic abilities and goals without regard to how much it costs.
3. Students should be assured that if they complete their work satisfactorily, they will be able to complete their studies.

First, then, is the premise that it is primarily up to the families to pay for college. It's not about government handouts or free rides for everyone. It's first up to the family. And that's why in the previous chapter we spent all that time discussing ways for families to save and prepare for the upcoming college expenses.

But the key phrase is "to the extent they are able." Just because a family does not have the resources does not mean the children should be denied access to college.

As we pointed out very early on in this book, the benefits of an educated populace are enormous, and not just to the individual. Society benefits when more of its population is educated. Many years ago, our society agreed that everyone should have access to education through high school, and we mandated that every child attend high school (or at least be homeschooled). In today's society we know the importance of higher education. But rather than mandate that children attend college and make it free, we provide financial assistance to those who need it so that cost is not a barrier and society is not paying enormous sums to those who don't need it to attend college. But since having free tuition is not enough—students still have to buy books and be able to eat and have a roof over their heads—our society supports students attending college through federal, state, and local financial aid programs. Furthermore, unlike high school students, college students are adults, almost all whom are at least eighteen years old. Through our state taxes, society provides reduced tuition at the publically supported colleges. This commitment to the state college systems began in the mid-1800s with a few states and has grown to now include all states. If students were to pay the full cost of their education at a state college, the amount they'd have to pay would be significantly higher. But we've set up the state colleges to get much of their funding from the state tax coffers, thus reducing the costs to all residents of the state.

Essentially, then, if a family cannot afford to send a child to college, there are financial aid programs that will supplement the family's ability to pay, thus providing access to college. In addition, there are lower-cost alternatives that states created to serve residents.

Second, we provide students with the choice of college by providing more money to students who have the greater need. A student who wants to attend a high-cost private college will qualify for more aid, thus reducing the out-of-pocket costs for the family. Although this commitment to providing students with choice has eroded, there are many colleges and universities where this is still the rule, not the exception. The choice may be a tougher one in some cases because the financial aid offered is in the form of more loans. But at least that money is available to students. And, it's important to note, many of the high-cost private colleges provide so much grant aid that students actually wind up borrowing less than they would at the lower-cost public colleges. That is why it is essential you don't eliminate any college from the list until you know how much you will be responsible for paying.

Finally, the third principle deals with persistence. If a student is progressing through college satisfactorily, that student should be able to complete his or her studies knowing that the financial aid awarded will not end after the first or second year. The student will still have to qualify, and if the family financial situation has changed, so might the financial aid award. In addition, the type of aid might change. For example, many colleges do not offer loans to first-year students because they believe that the first year is the most at-risk year. If a student has difficulty in school, for any number of reasons including personal ones, that student should not be overburdened. Students with just one year of college usually don't have the same access to quality high-paying jobs as do college graduates. Some colleges hold off on awarding loans to these students and phase in loans as the student progresses through school. Although this looks like a classic "bait and switch," it really is done with a great deal of thought and care to make sure students who don't get beyond their first year don't carry large amounts of loans.

That being said, it is a concern for many students and families, so you can ask the financial aid office about it when considering which college to attend. The question you would ask would simply be, Do you routinely package loans as part of your financial aid award? Then follow up about whether the school packages second-, third-, or fourth-year students differently.

CHAPTER 3

Financial Aid

Admission representatives recruit students; financial aid administrators recruit parents.

Catherine Thomas,
former director of financial aid,
University of Southern California.

More than two-thirds of college students receive some sort of financial aid to attend college. And the total amount of aid they received in 2015 was about $250 billion. Yes, you read that right: two hundred and fifty billion dollars. Furthermore, well over half of students receive so-called free money—that is, grants, scholarships, and tuition discounts totaling more than $120 billion. The total amount of funds taken out in loans was similar (about $115 billion), and that money went to a little more than a third of college students. It's not surprising, then, that the total outstanding student debt is more than a trillion dollars.

What these numbers show is just how extensive the commitment is to providing access to college for those who need assistance paying for school. What's extraordinary about the help is that, while there are multiple sources of this aid, the overwhelming percentage (69 percent) comes from federal and state governments. And that doesn't count the subsidy that students receive when they attend public colleges in their home state.

In this chapter, we'll discuss the types and sources of financial aid to help you gain a better understanding of what to expect when you apply for financial aid. Then later, we'll go through the step-by-step procedures you need to follow in order to qualify for this aid.

🎓 Need-Based Versus Merit-Based Aid

The first subject you need to understand is the concept of need-based versus merit-based aid. Almost all the federal financial aid programs are need-based and require one specific application. For the most part, state programs are also need-based, but many states also have a merit component that we'll discuss later. Whether institutional aid is merit- or need-based is totally up to the college itself; most colleges award both. Private scholarships also award both kinds, but generally more merit-based aid.

What do we mean by merit-based aid? Well, it's not just about top grades or high test scores. Merit can mean pretty much anything. For example, athletic scholarships are a kind of merit-based aid. So are scholarships awarded to a virtuoso violinist or an exceptional geek. Tuition discounts can be considered merit-based because that's how some colleges tempt students they most want by providing higher scholarships that are not based on need. Colleges may also use scholarships instead of less attractive awards (e.g., loans and work-study) for students they most want to attract. They may also award scholarships to the children of alumni to make the alumni happy (and perhaps inspire them to donate more). Colleges use scholarships in varying degrees and ways to help their enrollment. If a college is struggling to fill a class, or if the college wants to improve its reputation, it may try to "buy" the best and brightest. These colleges will likely be doing something similar with faculty by offering them higher wages or bonuses. It's an effective marketing tool and some bright or talented students can benefit greatly.

The point is that institutional scholarship money is discretionary. There is no absolute method of determining how they use their money—and it can change year to year—so the question we're most asked is, What schools should my child apply to so he or she can get the most in scholarships? It's tough to answer. The awarding of merit-based aid is often an admission decision, not a financial aid decision. As a very general rule, the lower the academic reputation, the more the college—at least for private colleges—is interested in attracting the best and brightest students by awarding merit-based aid. The rule does not apply to public colleges since those schools usually don't have that much of their own discretionary money to award and they're bound by public policy.

Therefore, once again I emphasize that choosing the right college should be based on all the key factors, with cost being only one consideration.

A word about ethnicity: One of the big myths is that financial aid is awarded based on ethnic or cultural criteria. Admittedly there are certainly some individual scholarships for which the donor specified that the recipient be a member of a particular group (e.g., a church-related scholarship may be awarded only to a member of that church who has exemplified the church's philosophy). But relative to the amount of money available, those scholarships represent only a very small piece of the pie. Ethnicity, race, religion, and other similar types of criteria do not play any part in government-based aid. Furthermore, there are legal issues surrounding admission based on race or ethnicity that have not yet been resolved. And it's quite possible that colleges use their institutional aid to attract minorities, just as they use their aid to attract the students they most want to enroll for a range of other reasons.

How Need Is Determined

Since most financial aid is awarded based on need, there must be a basis for determining that need. And indeed, there is. The formula for how need is determined is quite simple:

Total cost – the family's expected contribution = Need.

Since we've already looked at the total cost, the next question is how the family's expected contribution is determined. And here's where it starts to get complicated.

First, for federal aid, as we said early on, the underlying principle is that the primary responsibility of paying for a college education rests with the family *to the extent they are able*. That last phrase is the key, so there is a regulated need-analysis formula that calculates how much the family can afford. The formula known as the federal methodology (FM) tallies the family's income, adds a portion of the assets, adds a contribution from the student, and comes out with a figure called the expected family contribution (EFC). Many factors are considered in this formula, including the number of family members, the number of family members enrolled, the amount of assets, the amount of assets stashed away for the parents' retirement, and the age of the parents.

To make matters a bit more complicated, there is a second form of need analysis that some colleges use to award their own aid (and, as we pointed out, that amount is quite significant). The colleges that use this formula, the institutional methodology (IM), can also award federal aid using IM. IM uses more data elements to determine the family's ability to pay, and, because it is more complex, the expected family contribution from one is not always higher or lower than the other. IM takes into account other factors such as home equity and divorced/separated parent's income to give a more accurate reflection of the family's ability to pay.

To estimate your EFC using either or both formulas, you can go to one of several calculators available online. The best one I have found, and one that is almost always up-to-date and accurate, is the one produced by The College Board (it's no wonder it's more accurate: it is the organization responsible for determining the IM). You can find the calculator at The College Board website (https://bigfuture.collegeboard .org/pay-for-college/paying-your-share/expected-family -contribution-calculator).

🎓 Gift Aid Versus Self-Help Aid

One important way financial aid programs are different is whether the money you receive is gift aid—that is, money you don't have to either pay back or earn—or self-help aid, which you either must pay back or earn. Scholarships and grants, and tuition discounts for that matter, are forms of gift aid. Work-study and loans are self-help.

Most students pay for their schooling through a combination of gift aid, self-help aid, and the family contribution (EFC). Clearly you will want to maximize the portion of gift aid so you are not burdened with debt or the student does not have to work too many hours while also attending school.

But you and your child should be careful to put the ratio of gift to self-help aid into perspective. With regard to the work-study portion, studies have repeatedly demonstrated that working part-time in school actually helps students succeed, since these students are often better organized and more focused. But these same studies show that working too many hours—more than twenty per week—takes a toll on students. This is especially true for students in certain majors, since some of these subjects, such as art, architecture, music, and laboratory sciences, require many more hours of work or practice than other academic disciplines. Parents and their children should discuss expectations about the number of hours the student will work.

The same can be said of having to borrow more in order to attend the college the student prefers. As we said early on, cost and out-of-pocket expenses should be only one of many factors determining which college to attend. It's an important one, for sure, but the difference in price might be less than what you think. Rarely does a student or the family pay the sticker price for college and, as we have said, often the highest-priced colleges award the most gift aid, sometimes reducing the cost to the family to less than the out-of-pocket cost at a public college.

Types of Gift Aid

Gift aid consists of any money that is given to students that they don't have to pay back or work for. Obviously, then, this is the best type of aid. According to The College Board, it makes up 47 percent of all aid awarded ("Trends in Student Aid 2015").

Institutional Grants and Scholarships
Most colleges offer gift aid from their own resources. They can be called scholarships or grants, or sometimes just "tuition discount," and they can either be merit-based or need-based. Most colleges award both. In fact, institutional grants and scholarships makes up 42 percent of the gift aid awarded to students ("Trends in Student Aid 2015"). The criteria for eligibility vary from college to college, but if a student has demonstrated need and is eligible for federal aid, the amount

of these institutional funds is tied into the amount of federal aid awarded. Institutional grants are very competitive, particularly if they are merit-based. They may be awarded only to full-time students, to those who apply by a particular deadline, to students with higher grades, or to students fitting any particular criterion the college wishes to base its award on. It can be almost impossible to determine the criteria the college uses since these funds are often used to help attract the students the college most wants to enroll. Using the college's net price calculator can give you some insight, but those are averages, not individual awards. And note that some schools may require a separate scholarship application in addition to the usual financial aid application(s).

State Grants and Scholarships

Every state has some sort of grant program administered by the state, and the total amount is about $10 billion (NASSGAP Annual Survey, 2013–14). Some of these are merit-based, some are need-based, and some are a combination of the two in which the student must have demonstrated need but qualifies for a larger grant based on grades or test scores. You must be a resident of the state and, for the most part, attending a college in that state. There are a few exceptions, such as in New England, where a student from one state can attend a college in a neighboring state and qualify for a state grant. There is usually no separate application, but for some states you must specify on the Free Application for Federal Student Aid (FAFSA) that you are also applying for a state grant, and in a few states there is a supplemental application. Check with your individual state grant agency to make sure so you don't miss out on these grants.

Federal Pell Grant
(https://studentaid.ed.gov/sa/types/grants-scholarships/pell)
The Federal Pell Grant is by far the largest single grant program, with more than eight million students receiving some

$30 billion annually. Pell Grants are strictly need-based and target students from the lowest income groups. A student from family of four with one child in college would qualify for a Pell Grant if the total family income is lower than around $50,000. The maximum Pell Grant for the 2016–17 academic year is $5,815 per year, and that assumes the student is attending full-time for two semesters or three quarter terms. Part-time students receive proportionally less. Pell Grants are portable, meaning that if you qualify, you can go to a different college and get the same amount. The amount you receive is not dependent on the cost of education, since every college costs more than the maximum Pell Grant.

Federal Supplemental Educational Opportunity Grant
(FSEOG; https://studentaid.ed.gov/sa/types/grants
-scholarships/fseog)
This program, generally referred to either as FSEOG or as Supplemental Grant, is a campus-based program, and the amount awarded to students is up to the college itself. The grant goes mostly to Pell Grant recipients, so it also targets students with the lowest income. Relative to other grant programs, it is tiny, totaling only about $600 million. The average supplemental grant is about $550, which means only a little more than one million students receive it. Still, you might see the grant on your award letter. And since it is given to the colleges in a lump sum, the colleges can use it to help needy students at their own discretion.

Other Federal Grants
There are several other, smaller grant programs with specific designations that are worth mentioning. One is the Teacher Education Assistance for College and Higher Education (TEACH) Grant (https://studentaid.ed.gov/sa/types/grants -scholarships/teach) awarded to students enrolled in or planning to enroll in coursework in preparation for a career as a

teacher. There are specific requirements, and if the student does not become a teacher, the grant converts to a loan.

A second federal grant program is the Iraq and Afghanistan Service Grant (https://studentaid.ed.gov/sa/types/grants-scholarships/iraq-afghanistan-service), which is awarded to children of service members who died as a result of their military service performed in Iraq or Afghanistan after the events of 9/11.

Private and Foundation Scholarships

One of the big myths about scholarships is that students don't take advantage of the millions of dollars out there that are available. False! For one, most of that hype refers to potential sources of scholarship, including employee benefits. Many employers provide funds for employees and children of employees to attend college. And they don't impose a limit. But if no employee applies for the benefit, then of course it's sitting out there unused. The same can be said of local foundation and charity scholarships. If your church group talks about having a program to help the members of the church but no one actually applies for the grant, then that is also counted as unused.

Second, this myth also usually includes federal, state, and institutional funds and even veterans benefits that go unused. Obviously not every veteran goes to college, even if he or she is eligible to receive a benefit.

That said, there are, in fact, millions of dollars in scholarship aid available to thousands of students. The good news is that it is relatively simple to access most of these scholarships. The bad news is that they are very competitive and also require very specific eligibility criteria. For example, there may be a scholarship available from a particular donor requiring that the recipient be from a specific hometown and have a specific major. If no one from Anytown, USA, attends XYZ University and majors in underwater basket weaving, then obviously that scholarship will go unused. Furthermore, if you are from that town, attend that university, and major in that field, you may still have to apply for it using a very specific application that requires you to write the equivalent of an entire term paper. And the grant may be for $100, which may not really be worth the trouble. And even if you do get the scholarship, if you are already receiving other financial aid, that other aid will have to be reduced because no student who receives financial aid can get more than the cost of education.

Still, we do recommend that you use one of the free scholarship searches and check out the possibilities. There are some $46 million dollars awarded by organizations to students, and while some of these can be extraordinarily difficult to get, someone is getting it, so why not you? The key is to pick and choose.

You should go through one of the scholarship search engines, identify the most likely scholarships, and apply, provided the application isn't so burdensome that it's not worth the time.

Then speak directly with your local church group and service organization (e.g., Rotary, Lions Club, Elks, etc.). Those organizations often award small scholarships, but the applications don't require too much effort.

Here are several free scholarship search programs that are worth checking out. Most of them use the same database, but occasionally there are individual differences. Under no circumstance should you ever pay to have a search done for you.

College Board (https://bigfuture.collegeboard.org/
    scholarship-search)
Fastweb (http://www.fastweb.com)
Scholarships.com (https://www.scholarships.com)
Scholarship Experts (https://www.scholarshipexperts
    .com)

🎓 Veterans Benefits
(http://www.benefits.va.gov/gibill/education_programs.asp)

Although veterans benefits would not normally be considered financial aid, they are, in a sense, grants for veterans and their dependents to attend college. The benefits also must be coordinated with other financial aid so the nonveterans benefit does not cause the recipient to receive more than the total educational cost. It's interesting to note that about a quarter of the recipients are not the veterans themselves but spouses and children of veterans.

There are a number of programs grouped under the veterans benefit umbrella:

Post-9/11 GI Bill: Under this program, recipients may receive reimbursement of the full year's tuition and fees for an in-state student at a public college and up to $21,085 at a private college (2015–16 rates) for up to 36 months. There may also be a monthly housing allowance and a books and supplies stipend. Veterans can transfer their eligibility to their spouse or dependent children.

Montgomery GI Bill: For active duty members of the military who enroll and contribute, the benefit will pay as much as $1,789 per month (2015) for full-time college or training. The benefits are not transferrable to family members.

Dependents Education Assistance Program (DEA): Eligible dependents of veterans who died or are permanently and totally disabled may receive up to $1,021 per month (2015).

For more information about Veterans Benefits, refer to the Veterans Administration (http://www.benefits.va.gov/gibill/education_programs.asp).

🎓 Work-Study

Work-study is a type of self-help aid for which the money must be earned through work. It differs from other part-time jobs in that a portion of the student's salary comes through the federal government and the hours the student can work are limited by the amount of the work-study award.

Federal Work-Study

The Federal Work-Study program (https://studentaid.ed.gov/sa/types/work-study) is a campus-based program in which federal funds go directly to the college to disburse as it sees fit. Recipients must qualify for need-based aid under the federal guidelines. Students work at part-time jobs, usually on campus, although there are some off-campus jobs that the school sets up with private, nonprofit organizations or public agencies and some private for-profit organizations where the jobs must be relevant to the student's course of study. Students must earn at least the minimum wage and can work only as much as the total awarded amount. Employers, whether the college itself or other organizations, don't have to pay the full salary; the student's earnings are subsidized by the college's Federal Work-Study allocation.

State Work-Study Programs

Several states, including Colorado, Florida, Idaho, Indiana, Kansas, Kentucky, Minnesota, Montana, Nevada, New Mexico, Pennsylvania, Texas, and Washington have work-study programs funded through state taxes. Like the Federal Work-Study program, the state programs are administered by the colleges and have many of the same requirements. Generally students must not only attend a college in that state, but they also must be residents of the state to qualify. You apply for a state work-study award through the same application used for other state aid, which is generally the FAFSA plus a supplement. Check with the college or the state grant agency for more information.

Service-Related Aid

In years past, many government agencies and some employers would provide educational benefits in exchange for a commitment to work at the agency after graduation. Although very few private employers still do this, some government agencies have continued (or restarted) the practice.

For example, in exchange for agreeing to serve in the military, the army, navy, air force, and marines all have scholarship programs through which selected students participate in the Reserve Officers' Training Corp (ROTC; http://www.goarmy.com/rotc/high-school-students/four-year-scholarship.html; http://www.nrotc.navy.mil/scholarships.html; https://www.afrotc.com/scholarships). While in school, students undergo military training for a few hours each week and receive a scholarship plus an allowance. After graduation, you must agree to serve in that service for one to two years for each year you receive a scholarship (for a total of eight years for a four-year undergraduate degree). You can receive up to the total tuition at a public college, monthly stipends of up to $600, and a stipend for books and supplies. Not every school has an ROTC program and each ROTC program is not at every school. For more information about the programs and to see which school has which program, check with the college and/or the military branch of service that interests you.

Service Academies

There are five US service academies:

US Military Academy at West Point, New York (http://
www.westpoint.edu/SitePages/Home.aspx)

US Naval Academy in Annapolis, Maryland (http://
www.usna.edu/homepage.php)

US Air Force Academy in Colorado Springs, Colorado
(http://www.usafa.org)

US Coast Guard Academy in New London, Connecti-
cut (http://www.uscga.edu)

US Merchant Marine Academy in Kings Point, New
York (https://www.usmma.edu)

Although attending one of the service academies would
not generally be considered financial aid or a kind of grant
program, by attending these colleges, you do not pay any
tuition or room and board, and you also receive a stipend
for other costs such as books and supplies (and uniforms),
which makes it very much like a financial aid program.
Admission is, as one would expect, very, very competitive,
and if you enroll, you must agree to serve in active duty upon
graduation. Generally the commitment is for about five
years, although you might also have to serve in the reserves
for an additional three years.

For more information about attending one of these academies, refer directly to the colleges themselves.

Loans

For many students and families, borrowing to pay for college is a necessity, even with generous grant and scholarship

offers. And as we said early on in this book, for many students and families, it is a reasonable way to pay. But there are many types of loans and some that are much better than others. They offer better terms, both in the amount of interest paid, but also in the opportunities to defer or delay repayment. Here are the different loan programs.

Federal Loans

The William D. Ford Direct Loan program consists of four types of loans.

Direct Subsidized Loans (https://studentaid.ed.gov/sa/types/loans/subsidized-unsubsidized) are loans given directly to undergraduate students who have demonstrated need. The maximum amount available is $3,500 for first-year students, and that amount goes up to $4,500 in the second year and to $5,500 in the third and fourth years. They are called "subsidized" because interest does not accrue as long as the student remains enrolled at least half-time. Then, upon leaving school, the student has six months before they have to repay. Again, interest does not accrue for that period. The interest rate is determined annually, and for loans taken out during the 2015–16 year, the rate is 4.29 percent. There is also a loan fee of about 1 percent. Students apply for this loan using the FAFSA.

Direct Unsubsidized Loans (https://studentaid.ed.gov/sa/types/loans/subsidized-unsubsidized) are loans given directly to undergraduate students who do *not* demonstrate need, so any student can qualify. Like subsidized direct loans, the maximum amount available is $3,500 for first-year students, and that amount goes up to $4,500 in the second year and to $5,500 in the third and fourth year. If the student also qualifies for Direct Subsidized Loans, the total amount the student can borrow is $5,500 for the first year (of which no more than $3,500 can be subsidized loan), $6,500 for the second year (of which no more than $4,500 can be subsidized loan), and $7,500 for the third and fourth years (of which no more than $5,500 can be subsidized loan). They are called "unsubsidized" because interest *does* begin to accrue immediately after the funds are disbursed. Students can defer payments for six months after leaving school, but interest continues to accrue and gets capitalized. Like Direct Subsidized Loans, the interest rate is determined annually, and for loans taken out during the 2015–16 year, the rate is 4.29 percent. There is also a loan fee of about 1 percent. Clearly the Direct Unsubsidized Loan is not nearly as attractive as the subsidized loan, so students will want to maximize the amount of subsidized loans. Students apply for this loan using the FAFSA.

Direct PLUS Loans (https://studentaid.ed.gov/sa/types/loans/plus) are loans given to graduate students or the parents of undergraduate students. Borrowers do not have to qualify based on ability to pay as other loans usually require, but you cannot have an "adverse credit history," which means, among other criteria, that you cannot be delinquent on any loans you have, including those that are not student loans. Here's a link to the other criteria that define adverse credit history: (https://studentaid.ed.gov/sa/glossary#Adverse_Credit_History). You can borrow up to the total cost of education minus any financial aid the student receives. The interest rate on loans disbursed during the 2015–16 year is 6.84 percent, and the interest rate is fixed for the life of the loan. There is also a loan fee that varies, but for loans made before October 1, 2016, that fee is 4.272 percent. Interest begins to accrue immediately but you can defer payments while the student is enrolled and for six months after the student leaves school. Interest continues to accrue during deferment periods.

A Direct Consolidation Loan (https://studentaid.ed.gov/sa/repay-loans/consolidation) is a way to combine all your federal student loans into one loan. This allows you to make one monthly payment instead of multiple payments and usually saves you money. We will talk more about consolidation later when we discuss loan repayment and ways to reduce your debt.

The Federal Perkins Loan (https://studentaid.ed.gov/sa/types/loans/perkins) is a low-interest (5 percent) student loan for undergraduate students who have demonstrated need. Students apply for this loan using the FAFSA. It is a campus-based program, so the college itself is the lender, not the federal government, and repayment generally goes to the school itself or to a servicer the school contracts with. Not all schools participate in the Perkins Loan program, and the amount of money you can borrow depends on how much the school has. The maximum is $5,500 per year, but most schools award considerably less. There are no other fees for Perkins Loans. You have a nine-month "grace period," which means you do not begin repaying this loan until nine months after you leave school. Interest does *not* accrue while you are in school or during your grace period.

State Loans

Eight states have their own loan programs totaling about $360 million per year. Although this is a small amount relative to the federal loan, it is significant enough to include here. Some of the terms of the loans are comparable to federal loans and some are not as good. In particular, be sure they offer an income-based repayment plan or something similar. But if you are a resident of and attend a college in one of the states with a program, it would be worth your while to investigate the loan program offered. You can also check with the financial aid office at the college itself. The eight states that have a program in 2015–16 are Alaska, Hawaii, Massachusetts, Minnesota, New Jersey, Texas, Washington, and Wisconsin, and the interest rates range from about 3.5 percent to 6.5 percent.

Institutional Loans

Many colleges offer their own loan program either as a supplement to the federal loans or as a more attractive substitute. The terms are determined by the colleges themselves and may or may not be as attractive as the federal loans. In particular, the repayment terms may not be as good and may not offer as many options for repayment. It's unlikely the institutional loan will offer income-based repayment plans. But you should check with your individual college to see whether they offer a loan, and if they do, whether the terms are as good as the federal loans.

CHAPTER 4

Applying for Financial Aid

The financial aid application process is streamlined: no more using estimated income information. Most students will be able to use an IRS data match to report income. Also, the financial aid and admission application processes are now more aligned. You can apply around the same time, making your decisions easier.

Students applying for financial aid for the 2017–18 academic year will be the first to experience big changes. For the first time, students do not have to wait until after January 1 to apply for aid. They can begin October 1, which means the timing is now closely aligned with the application for admissions. For example, students applying for admission to college for fall 2018 would normally have begun their admission process almost a year earlier—in the fall of 2017. But they couldn't have begun the financial aid process until after January 2018. Now they can begin both application processes at the same time.

In addition, and this may be the biggest change of all, the base year used to determine financial aid eligibility is no longer the year just prior to enrolling—that is, 2017 for a fall 2018 enrollment. Financial aid will now be based on the prior-prior year—that is, family income from 2016. This means that applicants will not have to use estimated values because their taxes were filed months before the financial aid application process begins. Furthermore, because taxes were filed much earlier, most students will be able to use the IRS data match rather than having to key in the income data.

With those two big shifts in mind, let's go through the financial aid process step-by-step. It's still not simple, and there are many potential roadblocks along the way. But those two changes, along with some other smaller modifications, have made it easier for most students.

First of all, you have two decisions to make.

Decision One

The first decision you need to make before applying for finan-cial aid is about the schools where you will apply for admis-sion. That seems obvious, but what you may not know is that while all colleges require financial aid applicants to complete the Free Application for Federal Student Aid (FAFSA), some colleges require a second application called the CSS PRO-FILE administered by The College Board (www.collegeboard .org). The PROFILE application, an online application only, is required by many of the private colleges as well as some of the larger public colleges—in particular, the flagship state colleges.

Decision Two

Once you have decided to which colleges you'll be applying, you then have to determine whether they require the PROFILE.

You can find this information either from the college's own website, brochures, or other written materials or by checking The College Board website, which lists all the colleges that require PROFILE (https://profileonline.collegeboard.org/prf/PXRemotePartInstitutionServlet/PXRemotePartInstitutionServlet.srv?excmpid=MTG336-ST-1-a20).

🎓 Completing the FAFSA

Beginning on October 1 of the year prior to your enrollment, you can begin the process of applying for financial aid. Completing the FAFSA initiates this process. The FAFSA is the only form allowed to establish eligibility for federal financial aid, even if you also have to fill out the PROFILE.

Most students complete the FAFSA online (FAFSA on the Web, or FOTW), although there is also a paper copy that can be completed in some cases. Because of the potential delays involved, plus the built-in edit checks that eliminate many of the most common errors and the smart logic that omits questions irrelevant to your situation, it is highly recommended that you complete the form online. FOTW also allows you to take advantage of the IRS data retrieval so you don't have to enter your income information. To complete the application, go to FAFSA.ed.gov (https://fafsa.ed.gov/).

> Let me underscore that you should not have to pay anyone to complete the FAFSA for you. It is free; there is a great deal of free help available, including online and by phone; and you can even ask financial aid professionals questions about specific issues. Anyone who guarantees you will get "more" financial aid if he or she completes complete the application for you is not legitimate. So beware of scams.

Getting Started

You can start applying for federal student aid beginning October 1 of the year before your expected enrollment. Before you get started, however, you need to prepare. Find and have handy the following:

- student's Social Security Number
- student's driver's license number
- alien registration card (i.e., "green card") if the student is an eligible noncitizen
- parent's Social Security Number
- records of any nontaxable income
- parent's current bank and brokerage account statements
- student's current bank and brokerage account statements

In addition, in the Appendix is a copy of the FAFSA on the Web worksheet. This worksheet previews the questions you'll be asked on the FAFSA and provides some important information you will need during the financial aid process.

On the next few pages, we will show each of the screens you'll need to complete when submitting the FAFSA on the Web. Note that smart logic is used, so you won't see questions that are irrelevant to you (e.g., if you don't report that you have a second parent living with you, you will not be asked about the second parent's income). You also will not be able to move to the next screen until you have answered all the required questions, and you'll get an error message with the skipped question or unaccepted answer highlighted.

When you first visit FAFSA.ed.gov, you will be greeted with the welcome screen where you can get started.

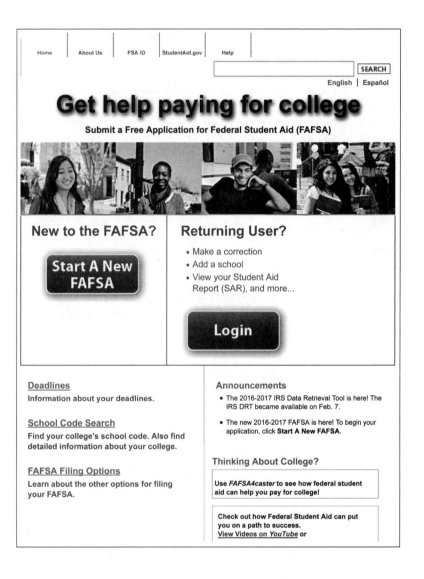

Your first task will be to create a login:

Login

Student Information

Form Approved
OMB No. 1845-0001
App. Exp. 12/31/2017

Instructions are provided for each FAFSA question in the Help and Hints section on the right side of the page and are also available by clicking **Need Help?** at the bottom of the page. Enter either your (the student's) FSA ID or personal information to log in to *FAFSA on the Web*.

○ Enter your (the student's) FSA ID   ● Enter the student's information

Do not log in with the FSA ID if you are not the student.
The student's first name

The student's full last name

The student's Social Security Number
From a Freely Associated State?

The student's date of birth (mmddyyyy)

OR

If you don't have a login (FSA ID), you can enter the student's information and create a login on a later screen where you see "Create a FSA ID." When you click that, you'll see this screen:

Create a New FSA ID

An FSA ID gives you access to Federal Student Aid's online systems and can serve as your legal signature.

Only create an FSA ID using your own personal information and for your own exclusive use. You are not authorized to create an FSA ID on behalf of someone else, including a family member. Misrepresentation of your identity to the federal government could result in criminal or civil penalties.

To create your own personal FSA ID, enter answers for the questions below and select CONTINUE.

Important: When you are done click the CANCEL button to clear your data, even if you did not finish creating your FSA ID. Just closing your browser window or going to another website may not be enough to prevent other people using this computer from seeing your information until the session expires.

By scrolling down, you'll then see:

* Required

Create An FSA ID (/npas/index.htm#register)

Edit My FSA ID (/npas/index.htm#edit)

E-mail   ❷ (/npas /index.htm)

Confirm E-mail   ❷ (/npas /index.htm)

Username ⁎   ❷ (/npas /index.htm)

Password ⁎   ❷ (/npas /index.htm)

✔ Numbers ✔ Uppercase Letters ✔ Lowercase Letters ✔ Special Characters ✔ 8-30 Characters ☐ Show Text

Confirm Password ⁎   ❷ (/npas /index.htm)

Are you 13 years of age or older? ⁎ ⚪ I am 13 years of age or older.   ❷ (/npas /index.htm)
⚪ I am 12 years of age or younger.

CONTINUE ›

⁎ Edit My FSA ID (/npas/index.htm)

⁎ Frequently Asked Questions (/npas/pub/faq.htm)

This is a U.S. Federal Government owned computer system, for the use by authorized users only. Unauthorized access violates Title 18, U.S. Code Section 1030 and other applicable statutes. Violations are punishable by civil and criminal penalties. Use of this system implies consent to have all activities on this system monitored and recorded, which can be provided as evidence to law enforcement officials.

This allows you to log back in at any time. When you then move on, you get to the school selection screen on which you designate to which schools you will be applying. You also can select whether you will be living on campus, off campus, or with your family. You can select as many as ten schools. Once you select the schools, you can reorder them by using the First/Up/Down/Last buttons. If you don't know the Federal School Code, you can use the search function.

School Selection Summary

For each school listed, select the appropriate housing plan from the dropdown list.

You may change the positioning of any school in this list. To do so, click on the school name and then use the buttons on the right to change the position of the selected school. The **FIRST** and **LAST** buttons will move the school to either the top or bottom of your list, and the **UP** and **DOWN** buttons will move the school one position up, or one position down.
For federal student aid purposes, it does not matter in what order you list your selected schools. However, the order in which you list schools may affect your eligibility for state aid. Find more information on your state's preferences for listing schools here.

School Name	Federal School Code	Housing Plans	
COLLEGE OF WILLIAM & MARY	003705	On Campus	Remove
UNIVERSITY OF VIRGINIA - SFS	003745	On Campus	Remove

FIRST   UP   **DOWN**   **LAST**

VIEW SELECTED SCHOOL INFORMATION

ADD A SCHOOL
Processing

Following this, you then get to the student demographic screens, which are self-explanatory.

Student Demographic Information

Your last name
Student

Your first name
New

Your middle initial

Your Social Security Number
987-65-4321

Your date of birth (mmddyyyy)
01/01/1998

Are you male or female?
○ Male   ○ Female

Your permanent mailing address (include apt. number)

Your city (and country if not U.S.)

Your state
Select

Your ZIP code

Have you lived in your state for at least 5 years?
○ Yes   ○ No

Your telephone number

Your e-mail address

What is your marital status as of today?
Select

Do you have driver's license information that you want to provide?
○ Yes   ● No

Processing

Student Eligibility

Are you a U.S. citizen?

Select

Are you registered with the Selective Service System?

○ Yes   ○ No

What will your high school completion status be when you begin college in the 2016-2017 school year?

Select

What will your grade level be when you begin the 2016-2017 school year?

Select

What degree or certificate will you be working on when you begin the 2016-2017 school year?

Select

Are you interested in being considered for work-study?

Select

Will you have your first bachelor's degree before you begin the 2016-2017 school year?

○ Yes   ○ No

Are you a foster youth or were you at any time in the foster care system?

Select

Highest school completed by Parent 1

Select

Highest school completed by Parent 2

Select

Student Eligibility continued

Enter the name, city, and state of your high school, then click **Confirm**.
What is the name of your high school?

In what city is your high school located?

In what state is your high school located?

Select

CONFIRM

Processing

Next you get to select the colleges you want to receive the information on your FAFSA. You can either put in the Federal School Code if you know it (most of the colleges list it on their brochures and websites) or you can do a search. Note that sometimes a college with the name "The College of . . ." will be listed under *T* alphabetically.

School Selection

You can add up to 10 colleges to your FAFSA. If you know your college's school code, use the option to the right to search. If you need help finding your college, use the state (required), city (optional), and school name (optional) fields to begin your search.

All of the information you include on your FAFSA, with the exception of the list of colleges, will be sent to each of the colleges you list. In addition, all of your FAFSA information, including the list of colleges, will be sent to your state student grant agency.

State

    Select

City

(optional)
School Name

(optional)
SEARCH Search Tips
OR
Federal School Code

SEARCH

Processing

One of the nice features is the ability to do a side-by-side comparison of the schools you selected. As you can see in the sample below, not only do you see the basic details about each college, you see at a glance some of the key pieces of information that may help you decide which college to attend. Of course, you should look into the data closely—in particular, the net price average, which, as it says in the legend, is the "average yearly price . . . after deducting any grant and scholarship aid received." But graduation and retention rates are also important numbers because they may indicate the degree to which the college invests in your success. A high graduation rate speaks volumes not only about the kind of students who attend but also about the commitment the college makes to ensure that you see your goal to the end. The retention rate may also tell you about how students who start out there feel about the college. Since you have a choice of which college you want to attend, high retention rates and low transfer rates, even if the numbers are averages and impersonal, mean that students appear to be happy at that school. Couple those with a high graduation rate and you get exactly the kind of college you're looking for.

Compare School Information

The following information is a subset of data that has been obtained from the *College Navigator* Web site, developed by the National Center for Education Statistics. Complete information for each college can be accessed by visiting College Navigator

School Name:	COLLEGE OF WILLIAM & MARY	UNIVERSITY OF VIRGINIA - SFS
Address:	P.O. BOX 8795	1847 UNIVERSITY AVENUE
City:	WILLIAMSBURG	CHARLOTTESVILLE
Federal School Code:	003705	003745
Web site:	www.wm.edu	www.virginia.edu/
School Type:	4-year, Public	4-year, Public
Tuition and Fees:		
In-State	$17,656	$13,208
Out-of-State	$39,916	$42,394
Net Price Average:	$12,406	$14,069
Graduation Rate:	90%	94%
Retention Rate:	95%	97%
Transfer Rate:	8%	4%
Additional Information from *College Navigator*:	NA	NA

- The information provided above is updated quarterly and may not reflect recent changes.
- If you are attending a branch campus, the information provided here may be for the main campus. *College Navigator* may have more specific information.
- The amounts for tuition and fees apply to full-time, first-time degree/certificate-seeking students.
- **Net Price Average** is the average yearly price charged to full-time, first-time undergraduate students receiving student aid at an institution of higher education after deducting any grant and scholarship aid received. Average Net Price provides students and families with an idea of how much a first-time, full-time undergraduate student who receives grant/scholarship aid pays to attend a particular institution after subtracting out that grant/scholarship aid.
- **Graduation rate** is the percentage of a school's first-time, first-year undergraduate students who complete their program within 150% of the published time for the program.
- **Retention rate** is the percentage of a school's first-time, first-year undergraduate students who continue at that school the next year.
- **Transfer rate** is the percentage of a school's first-time, first-year undergraduate students who transfer to another college within 150% of the published time for the program.
- NA indicates that information is not available from *College Navigator*.

Now, as you move onto the next section of FAFSA on the Web, you get into questions about who you are and whose income will be considered when need-based financial aid is awarded. Earlier in this book, I pointed out that one of the basic tenets of federal financial aid is that the family has the primary responsibility for paying for the undergraduate education of each of the family members. But clearly, that applies only up to a certain point. Should parents always have the responsibility? What about when the student is forty years old? I think we can all agree that the parents of a forty-year-old should no longer have the responsibility. Okay, then, what about age thirty? Or age twenty-five? At what age does the student become totally responsible? The federal aid system defines independence as students who are twenty-four years old, single, have no children of their own, and have not served in the military.

But, you might argue, "Even though I'm only eighteen, my parents refuse to pay. I don't live with them and they don't provide any money for me." Who should pay in this situation? Obviously you, to the extent you can. But that won't be enough. Then who pays? My answer to that is—not me! Just because your parents don't want to pay, why would you expect me, and millions of other taxpayers, to pay?

That is probably why, except for situations where the student is truly estranged, the federal government has determined that taxpayers do not have the responsibility to pay for the undergraduate education of anyone who is single, under age twenty-four, with no children, and not a veteran.

Dependency Determination

Were you born before January 1, 1993?
○ Yes ● No

As of today, are you married?
○ Yes ● No

At the beginning of the 2016-2017 school year, will you be working on a master's or doctorate program (such as an MA, MBA, MD, JD, PhD, EdD, or graduate certificate, etc.)?
○ Yes ● No

Do you now have or will you have children who will receive more than half of their support from you between July 1, 2016 and June 30, 2017?
○ Yes ○ No

Do you have dependents (other than your children or spouse) who live with you and who receive more than half of their support from you, now and through June 30, 2017?
○ Yes ○ No

Using the smart logic built into the FOTW program, the system will make a determination about your dependency status, and if you are considered dependent, you will be required to fill in your parents' financial information.

If you are unable to provide parental information, additional information will be required, including documentation about any special circumstance. In these situations, the financial aid administrator at the college has the authority to decide whether to require parental data. But as I stated above, parental refusal or unwillingness to provide the data is not considered a special circumstance. Without parental information, dependent students can complete the FOTW but will only be eligible for an unsubsidized loan.

Dependency Status Results

Based on your answers to the dependency status questions, **you are considered a dependent student. This means you must provide parental information.** Select "I will provide parental information" and click **Next** to continue to Parent Demographics.

If you have a special circumstance and are unable to provide parental information, under very limited circumstances, you may be able to submit your FAFSA without parental information. Select "I am unable to provide parental information" and click **Next** to get additional information.

- ⦿ I will provide parental information
- ○ I am unable to provide parental information

Assuming your parents will provide their information, the next screens you see will be the parent demographics screens:

Parent Demographics Information

As of today, what is the marital status of your legal parents (biological and/or adoptive)?
[Select ▾]

Your parents' e-mail address
[   ]

Have your parents lived in Virginia for at least 5 years?
○ Yes   ○ No

Your parents' number of family members in 2016-2017 (household size)

If you are not sure who is considered a family member, click **Household Size** to answer the questions on the worksheet.

[   ]

[HOUSEHOLD SIZE]

How many people in your parents' household will be college students between July 1, 2016 and June 30, 2017? Do not include your parents.

[   ]

Processing

These are then followed by the parent financial screens. On these screens, you can have the IRS Date Retrieval Tool transfer your parents' tax return information from the IRS to the FAFSA. You also have to answer additional questions about nontaxable income and assets.

Parent Tax Information

For 2015, have your parents completed their IRS income tax return or another tax return?
[Select ▾]

Parent Tax Information

For 2015, have your parents completed their IRS income tax return or another tax return?

Already completed ⬍

For 2015, what is your parents' tax filing status according to their tax return?

Married-Filed Joint Return ⬍

⚪ To determine if you, the parents, can use the IRS Data Retrieval Tool to transfer your tax return information from the IRS into the FAFSA, **answer the following question(s):**

Did you, the parents, file a Form 1040X amended tax return?
⚪ Yes ⚫ No

Did you, the parents, file a Puerto Rican or foreign tax return?
⚪ Yes ⚫ No

Did you, the parents, file taxes electronically in the last 3 weeks (or by mail in the last 11 weeks)?
⚪ Yes ⚫ No

Based on your response, we recommend that you, the parents, transfer your information from the IRS into this FAFSA. How you filed your taxes can affect whether your tax return information is available to transfer.

Enter your FSA ID and click **Link To IRS**.
Which parent are you?

Select ⬍

What is your (the parent's) FSA ID?
FSA ID Username or Verified E-mail Address

FSA ID Password

- Create an FSA ID
- Forgot Username
- Forgot Password

LINK TO IRS

Parent Financial Information

What type of income tax return did your parents file for 2015?

Select ⬍

What was your parents' adjusted gross income for 2015?
$|_____|.00

INCOME ESTIMATOR

How much did your Parent 1 (father/mother/stepparent) earn from working (wages, salaries, tips, etc.) in 2015?
$|_____|.00

How much did your Parent 2 (father/mother/stepparent) earn from working (wages, salaries, tips, etc.) in 2015?
$|_____|.00

As of today, is either of your parents a dislocated worker?

Select ⬍

Processing

Parent Financial Information continued

Enter the amount of your parents' income tax for 2015. This amount is found on IRS Form 1040-lines (56 minus 46).

$ [   ] .00

Enter your parents' exemptions for 2015. This amount is found on IRS Form 1040-line 6d.

[   ]

Did your parents have any of the following items in 2015? Check all that apply and provide amounts.

Additional Financial Information
☐ *American Opportunity Tax Credit* or *Lifetime Learning Tax Credit*
☐ Child support paid
☐ Taxable earnings from Work-study, Assistantships or Fellowships
☐ College grant and scholarship aid reported to the IRS
☐ Combat pay or special combat pay
☐ Cooperative education program earnings

Untaxed Income
☐ Payments to tax-deferred pension and retirement savings plans
☐ IRA deductions and payments to self-employed SEP, SIMPLE and Keogh
☐ Child support received
☐ Tax exempt interest income
☐ Untaxed portions of IRA distributions
☐ Untaxed portions of pensions
☐ Housing, food, and other living allowances paid to military, clergy, and others
☐ Veterans noneducation benefits
☐ Other untaxed income not reported such as workers' compensation or disability benefits

As of today, does the total amount of your parents' current <u>assets</u> exceed $18,300.00?
○ Yes   ○ No

Parent Financial Information continued

Enter the amount of your parents' income tax for 2015. This amount is found on IRS Form 1040-lines (56 minus 46).

$ [   ] .00

Enter your parents' exemptions for 2015. This amount is found on IRS Form 1040-line 6d.

[   ]

Did your parents have any of the following items in 2015? Check all that apply and provide amounts.

Additional Financial Information
☐ *American Opportunity Tax Credit* or *Lifetime Learning Tax Credit*
☐ Child support paid
☐ Taxable earnings from Work-study, Assistantships or Fellowships
☐ College grant and scholarship aid reported to the IRS
☐ Combat pay or special combat pay
☐ Cooperative education program earnings

Untaxed Income
☐ Payments to tax-deferred pension and retirement savings plans
☐ IRA deductions and payments to self-employed SEP, SIMPLE and Keogh
☐ Child support received
☐ Tax exempt interest income
☐ Untaxed portions of IRA distributions
☐ Untaxed portions of pensions
☐ Housing, food, and other living allowances paid to military, clergy, and others
☐ Veterans noneducation benefits
☐ Other untaxed income not reported such as workers' compensation or disability benefits

As of today, does the total amount of your parents' current <u>assets</u> exceed $18,300.00?
◉ Yes   ○ No

As of today, what is your parents' total current balance of cash, savings, and checking accounts?
$ [   ] .00
As of today, what is the net worth of your parents' investments, including real estate (not your parents' home)?
$ [   ] .00
As of today, what is the net worth of your parents' current businesses and/or investment farms?
$ [   ] .00

Next, the student will have to provide income information.

Student Tax Information

For 2015, have you completed your IRS income tax return or another tax return?

| Select |

Student Financial Information continued

Did you have any of the following items in 2015? Check all that apply and provide amounts.

Additional Financial Information
☐ Child support paid

☐ Taxable earnings from Work-study, Assistantships or Fellowships

☐ College grant and scholarship aid reported to the IRS

☐ Combat pay or special combat pay

☐ Cooperative education program earnings

Untaxed Income
☐ Payments to tax-deferred pension and retirement savings plans

☐ Child support received

☐ Housing, food, and other living allowances paid to military, clergy, and others

☐ Veterans noneducation benefits

☐ Other untaxed income not reported such as workers' compensation or disability benefits

☐ Money received or paid on your behalf

As of today, what is your total current balance of cash, savings, and checking accounts?
$ _____ .00
As of today, what is the net worth of your investments, including real estate (not your home)?
$ _____ .00
As of today, what is the net worth of your current businesses and/or investment farms?
$ _____ .00
Processing

Finally, the next screens are where you get to electronically sign and then submit the application.

Sign & Submit

Are you a preparer?
○ Yes ◉ No

Student Signature

Student's Social Security Number

Student's last name

Student's date of birth

READ BEFORE PROCEEDING

By signing this application electronically using your Federal Student Aid PIN, username and password, and/or any other credential or by signing a signature page and mailing it to us, YOU, THE STUDENT, certify that you:

1. will use federal and/or state student financial aid only to pay the cost of attending an institution of higher education,
2. are not in default on a federal student loan or have made satisfactory arrangements to repay it,
3. do not owe money back on a federal student grant or have made satisfactory arrangements to repay it,
4. will notify your school if you default on a federal student loan, and
5. will not receive a Federal Pell Grant from more than one school for the same period of time.

By signing this application electronically using your Federal Student Aid PIN, username and password, and/or any other credential or by signing a signature page and mailing it to us, you certify that all of the information you provided is true and complete to the best of your knowledge and you agree, if asked:

I, the student, agree to the terms outlined above.
○ Agree ◉ Disagree

What is your (the student's) FSA ID?Do not enter the FSA ID if you are not the student.
FSA ID Username or Verified E-mail Address

FSA ID Password

Don't have an FSA ID? Create an FSA ID. It takes only a few minutes.
Other options to sign and submit

Parent Signature

Are you signing as the student's Parent 1 (father/mother/stepparent), or Parent 2 (father/mother/stepparent)?

○ Parent 1 (Father/Mother/Stepparent) ○ Parent 2 (Father/Mother/Stepparent)

READ BEFORE PROCEEDING

By signing this application electronically using your Federal Student Aid PIN, username and password, and/or any other credential or by signing a signature page and mailing it to us, YOU, THE PARENT, certify that all of the information you provided is true and complete to the best of your knowledge and you agree, if asked:

1. to provide information that will verify the accuracy of your completed form
2. to provide U.S. or state income tax forms that you filed or are required to file.

You also certify that you understand that the Secretary of Education has the authority to verify information reported on your application with the Internal Revenue Service and other federal agencies.

If you sign this application or any document related to the federal student aid programs electronically using a PIN, username and password, and/or any other credential, you certify that you are the person identified by the PIN, username and password, and/or any

I, the parent, agree to the terms outlined above.
○ Agree ◉ Disagree

What is your (the parent's) FSA ID?
Do not enter the FSA ID if you are not the parent.
FSA ID Username or Verified E-mail Address

FSA ID Password

Create an FSA ID
Forgot Username
Forgot Password
Other options to sign and submit
Processing

For specific help on completing each question, refer to the online help offered on FOTW. You can also call the Federal Student Aid Information Center at 1-800-4-FED-AID (1-800-433-3243) or you can also get a free copy of the book *Filing the FAFSA*, a guide put together by EDvisors (https://www.edvisors.com/fafsa/book/user-info). This book is especially helpful for complicated family and financial situations.

The Next Step

A few days after you submit your FAFSA online, you will receive an e-mail directing you to a link to a Student Aid Report (SAR). The SAR summarizes what you filled out on your application. Review it to make sure the information is accurate. If it is not, you will have an opportunity to make corrections by following the instructions on the SAR.

That same information, in a different format, will be sent electronically to the schools you designated on the FAFSA. If you wish to designate additional schools, you can do so, again by following the instructions on the SAR.

If you filed your FAFSA on paper, you should get your SAR in the mail within about two weeks.

If, after a week, you do not receive a response after you submitted your FAFSA online, or two weeks if you filed on paper, you should call 1-800-4-FED-AID to check on the status. If you have any questions or concerns, you can call that same number for help.

At this point in the process, most communication will be done between the individual colleges and you. The only communication you will have with the processor of the FAFSA is if you need to make corrections or have the information sent to additional schools.

🎓 Completing the PROFILE

As we discussed earlier, many schools require an additional financial aid application, the CSS PROFILE. This form, administered by The College Board, is an online application that is available at https://student.collegeboard.org/css -financial-aid-profile.

The PROFILE asks additional questions about you and your family's finances, and it uses a different formula, the institutional methodology (IM), to calculate your family's expected contribution. Many colleges feel that by knowing more about your family, they have a better sense of the family's financial strength. They collect additional data not to limit awards but to better address the real financial needs of students and their families. They use this formula when awarding their own institutional funds because it goes into more depth and tells a much greater story about the family's real financial strength and ability to pay for college. That's why it's important to note that while sometimes the expected family contribution calculated using the federal methodology is lower than the one calculated using the IM, it's just as often the opposite. The decision of whether to use the data from the CSS PROFILE is an institutional decision, not the student's or the family's.

You can get an estimate of the results of the two different formulas by going to https://bigfuture.collegeboard.org/pay -for-college/paying-your-share/expected-family-contribution -calculator.

The CSS PROFILE

The first step in completing the PROFILE is to register. You do that by going to https://www.collegeboard.org and signing up. Once you've signed up, your information will be stored and you then register to complete the actual PROFILE application.

CollegeBoard.com

HELP DESK | CONTACT US | LOG OUT OF PROFILE

PROFILE Online 2016-17

REGISTRATION

? Student's Social Security Number: [ ] - [ ] - [ ]

Please enter your Social Security Number if you have one. Failure to provide an accurate Social Security Number can significantly delay the processing of your application by your college or program.

? Student's name:

[ ]   [ ]   [ ]
Last name (Family/Surname)   First name (Given)   Middle name

[ ]
? Preferred name

Student's title (optional):   ● Mr.   ○ Miss, Ms., or Mrs.

? Student's email address: [ ]

This email address will be used to communicate with you about PROFILE and the financial aid process, including PROFILE receipts, and, if required by your colleges and programs, the Noncustodial PROFILE and IDOC. This email address will only be shared with the colleges and programs to which you are applying. See Help if you are using an email filtering program and need information on how to receive College Board emails.

? Student's date of birth: [--Select a month--]   [--Select a day--]   [--Select a year--]
                                    Month   Day   Year

? Student's permanent address   [--Select a postal address--]
location:

[Back to Top]   [Continue]

CollegeBoard.com

HELP DESK | CONTACT US | LOG OUT OF PROFILE

PROFILE Online 2016-17

REGISTRATION

Student's permanent address: [ ]
                                  Address 1

                                  [ ]
                                  Address 2

                                  [ ]   [--Select a state--]   [ ]
                                  City   State   Zip code

Student's mailing address: [ ]
(If different from above)   Address 1

                                  [ ]
                                  Address 2

                                  [ ]   [--Select a state--]   [ ]
                                  City   State   Zip code

Student's preferred telephone number: [ ]   [ ] - [ ]
                                        Area code

[Back to Top]   [Previous] [Continue]

Now you get to select the colleges you want to receive the information. Note that the ID number is different than the Federal ID. Also, make sure note that you don't designate a college that doesn't request the CSS PROFILE (the smart logic in the program will not allow you to select a college that doesn't participate).

CollegeBoard.com

PROFILE Online 2016-17

HELP DESK   CONTACT US   LOG OUT OF PROFILE

COLLEGE AND PROGRAM SEARCH

Select the colleges and scholarship programs that you want to receive your PROFILE information. You may choose as many colleges and programs as you want, but you must select at least one college or scholarship program. You will be charged $16.00 per college or program selected. You can add or remove colleges or programs at any time before you submit your PROFILE application.

HOW TO SEARCH

Below there are three different ways to search for a college or program. **Use only one search method at a time.** Click the "Search" button to the right of your search method to see the results of your search. If you are interested in a college outside the U.S., you must search by the name or CSS Code Number of that college.

PRIORITY FILING DATES

Below each college or program name in the Search Results column will be any information provided by that college or program about its Priority Filing Dates. The Priority Filing Date is the date by which you should **submit** your completed PROFILE application. Your application will be processed immediately upon submission - the dates below are for information only.

INTERNATIONAL STUDENTS

[See More]

Search for colleges or programs using one of the following:

Search by a college's/program's CSS Code Number: SEARCH

Search by state (location of college/program):   -Select by state-   SEARCH

Search by college/program name: SEARCH

Search Results   **Selected Colleges/Programs**

ADD ►

To select a
recipient,
check it in
the list on
left and click
"Add"

◄ REMOVE

To remove a
recipient,
check it in
the list on
the right and
click
"Remove"

Click continue when you have finished your selection.

Once you have selected the colleges, the next screen will require that you choose where you will live when attending the school.

Finally, you will be asked about your parents and your family so the PROFILE can be tailored to you.

When you have completed the registration, you will then be able to start completing the PROFILE itself. Since this sample registered as a dependent student, the application starts by asking about the parents' information, income, and assets.

CollegeBoard.com

PROFILE Online 2016-17

| HELP DESK | CONTACT US | LOG OUT OF PROFILE |

SEARCH

APPLICATION

| Back to Registration | Back to Home Page | Add/Remove Colleges | Previous | Save & Continue |
| SAVE | SAVE & EXIT | | SUBMIT | PRINT/REVIEW APPLICATION |

GO TO SECTION: Select Section

STATUS: APPLICATION NOT SUBMITTED

Parents' Data (PD)

This section asks for information about the **student's parent(s) whose information is being given on this application**. If a question does not apply, you may leave it blank.

Help Code

	Field	Input	Code
	Parent 1 - Parent's relationship to the student	--Select an answer--	PD-100
	Name		PD-105
	Date of birth (MMDDYYYY)		PD-110
[?]	Is this parent self-employed or unemployed?	--Select an answer--	PD-115
	If this parent is unemployed enter the date unemployment began (MMDDYYYY)		PD-120
	Occupation		PD-125
	Employer		PD-130
	Number of years at current place of employment		PD-135
	Preferred daytime telephone number (######### - numbers only)		PD-140A
	This parent plans to draw Social Security upon retirement.	☐	PD-145
	This parent has a civil service or state sponsored retirement plan.	☐	PD-150
	This parent has a military sponsored retirement plan.	☐	PD-155
	This parent has a union or employer sponsored retirement plan.	☐	PD-160
	This parent has an IRA, Keogh, or other tax-deferred retirement plan.	☐	PD-165
	This parent has another retirement plan.	☐	PD-170
[?]	Enter the total current value of this parent's tax-deferred retirement, pension, annuity, and savings plans. Include IRA, SRA Keogh, SEP, 401(a), 401(k), 403(b), 408, 457, 501(c) plans, etc.		PD-175A
	What is the highest level of education this parent completed?	--Select an answer--	PD-178
	Will this parent attend college or university at least one term during the 2016-17 school year? (If so, complete the next question.)	--Select an answer--	PD-180
	What type of college or university will this parent attend?	--Select an answer--	PD-190

Parent 2 - Parent's relationship to the student

--Select an answer--   PD-195

Name   PD-200

Date of birth (MMDDYYYY)   PD-205

[?] Is this parent self-employed or unemployed?

--Select an answer--   PD-210

If this parent is unemployed enter date unemployment began
(MMDDYYYY)   PD-215

Occupation

PD-220

Employer

PD-225

Number of years at current place of employment   PD-230

Preferred daytime telephone number (######### - **numbers only**)   PD-235A

This parent plans to draw Social Security upon retirement.   ☐ PD-240

This parent has a civil service or state sponsored retirement plan. ☐ PD-245

This parent has a military sponsored retirement plan.   ☐ PD-250

This parent has a union or employer sponsored retirement plan.   ☐ PD-255

This parent has an IRA, Keogh or other tax-deferred retirement plan. ☐ PD-260

This parent has another retirement plan.   ☐ PD-265

[?] Enter the total current value of this parent's tax-deferred retirement,
pension, annuity, and savings plans. Include IRA, SRA Keogh, SEP,
401(a), 401(k), 403(b), 408, 457, 501(c) plans, etc.   PD-270A

What is the highest level of education this parent completed?

--Select an answer--   PD-273

Will this parent attend college or university at least one term during the
2016-17 school year? (If so, complete the next question.)   --Select an answer--   PD-275

What type of college or university will this parent attend?

--Select an answer--   PD-285

| SAVE | SAVE & EXIT | | SUBMIT | PRINT/REVIEW APPLICATION |

Back to Registration   Back to Home Page   Add/Remove Colleges   Previous   Save & Continue

CollegeBoard .com

PROFILE Online 2016-17

HELP DESK   CONTACT US   LOG OUT OF PROFILE

SEARCH

APPLICATION

Back to Registration   Back to Home Page   Add/Remove Colleges   ▌ Previous   Save & Continue

SAVE   SAVE & EXIT   SUBMIT   PRINT/REVIEW APPLICATION

GO TO SECTION: [Select Section ▼]

STATUS: APPLICATION NOT SUBMITTED

Parents' Household Information (PH)

This section asks for information about the **student's parents'** household. Any time a question says "you" or "your" it is referring to the student. Any time a question says "parents" it is referring to the student's parent(s) whose information is being given on this application. If the student's parents do not have an email address, you may leave that question blank.

Help Code

How many people are in your parents' household? **Always include yourself** (even if you do not live with your parents) **and your parent(s).** List their names and give information about them in Section FM (dependents) and Section PD (parents).

[   ]   PH-100A

How many people in your parents' household will be college students enrolled at least half-time between July 1, 2016 and June 30, 2017? **Do not include your parents.** Include yourself.

[   ]   PH-105A

What is your parents' state, territory, or province of legal residence?   [--Select an answer-- ▼]   PH-120

What is your parent's preferred email address?

[   ]   PH-125

At any time during 2014 or 2015 did your parent(s) receive Supplemental Nutrition Assistance Program (SNAP)/food stamp benefits?   [--Select an answer-- ▼]   PH-130

At any time during 2014 or 2015 did anyone in your parent(s) household receive free or reduced price lunch?   [--Select an answer-- ▼]   PH-131

At any time during 2014 or 2015 did your parent(s) receive Women, Infants and Children Program (WIC) benefits?   [--Select an answer-- ▼]   PH-132

As of today, are either of your parents a dislocated worker?   [--Select an answer-- ▼]   PH-135

SAVE   SAVE & EXIT   SUBMIT   PRINT/REVIEW APPLICATION

Back to Registration   Back to Home Page   Add/Remove Colleges   ▌ Previous   Save & Continue

CollegeBoard.com

HELP DESK   CONTACT US   LOG OUT OF PROFILE

PROFILE Online 2016-17

SEARCH

APPLICATION

Back to Registration   Back to Home Page   Add/Remove Colleges   Previous   Save & Continue

SAVE   SAVE & EXIT   SUBMIT   PRINT/REVIEW APPLICATION

GO TO SECTION: Select Section

STATUS: APPLICATION NOT SUBMITTED

Parents' 2015 Income & Benefits (PI)

This section asks for information about the student's parents' income and benefits for 2015. Any time a question says "you" or "your" it is referring to the student. Any time a question says "parents" it is referring to the student's parent(s) whose information is being given on this application. If a question does not apply, enter "0" (zero).

Help Code

Select your parents' tax filing status for the 2015 tax year.

--Select an answer--   PI-095

Enter the total number of exemptions your parents claimed for 2015 on their 2015 IRS Form 1040, line 6d.   PI-100A

Enter the 2015 wages, salaries, and tips your parents reported on their 2015 IRS Form 1040, line 7.   PI-105A

Enter the amount of taxable interest income your parents earned in 2015 as reported on their 2015 IRS Form 1040, line 8a.   PI-110A

Enter the amount of taxable dividend income your parents earned in 2015 as reported on their 2015 IRS Form 1040, line 9a.   PI-115A

Enter your parents' net income (or loss) from business, farm, rents, royalties, partnerships, estates, trusts, etc. as reported on their 2015 IRS Form 1040, lines 12, 17, and 18. To enter a loss, use a minus (-) sign.   PI-120A

Enter the total amount of your parents' other taxable income such as alimony received, capital gains (or losses), pensions, annuities, etc. as reported on their 2015 IRS Form 1040, lines 10, 11, 13, 14, 15b, 16b, 19, 20b and 21. To enter a loss, use a minus (-) sign.   PI-125A

Enter your parents' 2015 total adjustments to income claimed on their 2015 IRS Form 1040, line 36.   PI-130A

Enter your parents' 2015 adjusted gross income from their 2015 IRS Form 1040, line 37. To enter a loss, use a minus (-) sign.   PI-135A

Enter the income tax your parents paid for 2015 from their 2015 IRS Form 1040, line 56 minus line 46. (If a negative number, enter zero.)   PI-140A

Enter the Additional Medicare Tax your parents paid for 2015 from their 2015 IRS Form 8959, line 18. Enter 0 if Form 8959 was not filed.   PI-142A

Enter the amount of 2015 education credits (American Opportunity, Hope and Lifetime Learning) that your parents claimed on their 2015 IRS Form 1040, line 50.   PI-145A

Enter the amount of your parents' itemized deductions for 2015 from their 2015 IRS Schedule A, line 29. Enter "0" (zero) if they did not itemize deductions.   PI-150A

Enter the income parent 1 earned from work in 2015 from his or her 2015 IRS Form 1040, lines 7, 12, and 18 and IRS Schedule K-1 (Form 1065), Box 14 (Code A). If lines 12 or 18 or box 14 are negative, treat them as zero. If your parents filed a joint return, enter only parent 1's portion of lines 7, 12, and 18 and K-1, box 14. (Parent 1 is the parent you entered in PD-105.)   PI-155A

Enter the income parent 2 earned or expects to earn from work in 2015 from his or her 2015 IRS Form 1040, lines 7, 12, and 18 and IRS Schedule K-1 (Form 1065), Box 14 (Code A). If lines 12 or 18 or Box 14 are negative, treat them as zero. If your parents filed a joint return, enter only parent 2's portion of lines 7, 12, and 18 and K-1, box 14. (Parent 2 is the parent you entered in PD-195.) | PI-160A

Commissioned officers only - Enter the combat pay or special combat pay that your parents received for 2015 that was **taxable and included in your parents' adjusted gross income (AGI)** because one or both of them are commissioned officers. It is usually a portion of the amount reported in his or her W-2 Box 1. Do not enter untaxed combat pay reported in W-2 Box 12, Code Q. This does not apply to commissioned warrant officers. | PI-163A

[?] Enter the untaxed social security benefits your parents received or expect to receive for all family members **except you**, the student, in 2015. | PI-165A

[?] Enter the amount of Temporary Assistance for Needy Families (TANF) your parents received or expect to receive in 2015. | PI-175

[?] Enter the amount of child support your parents **received or expect to receive** for all children in 2015. (Do not enter the amount of child support they paid or expect to pay. Enter that amount in PE-100.) | PI-180A

[?] Enter the amount of deductible IRA and/or SEP, SIMPLE, or Keogh **payments** your parents made in 2015 as reported on their 2015 IRS Form 1040, lines 28 and 32. | PI-185A

Enter the untaxed portions of IRA distributions, excluding "rollovers," your parents **received** in 2015. These are reported on 2015 IRS Form 1040, lines 15a minus 15b. | PI-187A

[?] Enter the amount of **payments** (paid directly or withheld from earnings) to tax-deferred pension and savings plans your parents made or expect to make in 2015 including, but not limited to, amounts reported on W-2 Forms in Boxes 12a through 12d, codes D, E, F, G, H, and S. Include untaxed payments to 401(k) and 403(b) plans. | PI-190A

Enter the untaxed portion of pensions, excluding "rollovers," your parents **received** in 2015. These are reported on 2015 IRS Form 1040, lines 16a minus 16b. | PI-192A

[?] Enter the amount of the tuition and fees deduction your parents claimed on their 2015 IRS Form 1040 line 34. | PI-195A

[?] Enter the total amount withheld from your parents' wages in 2015 to contribute to a flexible spending account for medical expenses. | PI-200A

[?] Enter the total amount withheld from your parents' wages in 2015 to contribute to a flexible spending account for dependent care expenses. | PI-201A

[?] Enter the amount of the health savings account deduction your parents claimed on their 2015 IRS Form 1040 line 25. | PI-202A

[?] Enter the total amount withheld from your parents' wages in 2015 to contribute to a Health Savings Account (HSA). | PI-203A

[?] Enter the amount of Earned Income Credit your parents claimed on their 2015 IRS Form 1040, line 66a. | PI-205A

Enter the additional child tax credit your parents claimed on their 2015 IRS Form 1040, line 67. | PI-207A

[?] Enter the amount of housing, food, and other living allowances your parents received or expect to receive in 2015 from their employer or other sources as members of the military, clergy, or other profession. Include cash payments and cash value of benefits. Don't include the value of on-base military housing or the value of a basic military allowance for housing. | PI-210A

[?] Enter the value of on-base military housing or the value of the basic military allowance for housing your parents received or expect to receive in 2015 as members of the military. Include cash payments and cash value of benefits. | PI-211A

Enter the value of veterans' non-educational benefits such as Disability, Death Pension, or Dependency & Indemnity Compensation (DIC) or VA Educational Work-Study allowances your parents received or expect to receive in 2015. | PI-212A

[?] Enter the amount of tax-exempt interest income your parents received in 2015 as reported on their 2015 IRS Form 1040, line 8b. | PI-215A

[?] Enter the amount of foreign income exclusion your parents reported on their 2015 IRS Form 2555, line 45 or Form 2555EZ, line 18. | PI-220A

Enter the amount of cash your parents received and any money paid on their behalf (e.g., bills) in 2015. (Don't include child support or any other amounts reported elsewhere on this application.) | PI-230A

[?] Enter the amount of other untaxed income your parents received in 2015. See the worksheet for types of income to include and the instructions for types of income to exclude. Worksheet | PI-225A

SAVE   SAVE & EXIT   SUBMIT   PRINT/REVIEW APPLICATION

Back to Registration   Back to Home Page   Add/Remove Colleges   Previous   Save & Continue

CollegeBoard.com

PROFILE Online 2016-17

HELP DESK | CONTACT US | LOG OUT OF PROFILE

SEARCH

APPLICATION

Back to Registration | Back to Home Page | Add/Remove Colleges | Previous | Save & Continue

SAVE | SAVE & EXIT | SUBMIT | PRINT/REVIEW APPLICATION

GO TO SECTION: Select Section

STATUS: APPLICATION NOT SUBMITTED

Parents' 2015 Income & Benefits (PI)

This section asks for information about the student's parents' income and benefits for 2015. Any time a question says "you" or "your" it is referring to the student. Any time a question says "parents" it is referring to the student's parent(s) whose information is being given on this application. If a question does not apply, enter "0" (zero).

Help Code

Select your parents' tax filing status for the 2015 tax year.

--Select an answer-- PI-095

Enter the total number of exemptions your parents claimed for 2015 on their 2015 IRS Form 1040, line 6d. PI-100A

Enter the 2015 wages, salaries, and tips your parents reported on their 2015 IRS Form 1040, line 7. PI-105A

Enter the amount of taxable interest income your parents earned in 2015 as reported on their 2015 IRS Form 1040, line 8a. PI-110A

Enter the amount of taxable dividend income your parents earned in 2015 as reported on their 2015 IRS Form 1040, line 9a. PI-115A

Enter your parents' net income (or loss) from business, farm, rents, royalties, partnerships, estates, trusts, etc. as reported on their 2015 IRS Form 1040, lines 12, 17, and 18. To enter a loss, use a minus (-) sign. PI-120A

Enter the total amount of your parents' other taxable income such as alimony received, capital gains (or losses), pensions, annuities, etc. as reported on their 2015 IRS Form 1040, lines 10, 11, 13, 14, 15b, 16b, 19, 20b and 21. To enter a loss, use a minus (-) sign. PI-125A

Enter your parents' 2015 total adjustments to income claimed on their 2015 IRS Form 1040, line 36. PI-130A

Enter your parents' 2015 adjusted gross income from their 2015 IRS Form 1040, line 37. To enter a loss, use a minus (-) sign. PI-135A

Enter the income tax your parents paid for 2015 from their 2015 IRS Form 1040, line 56 minus line 46. (If a negative number, enter zero.) PI-140A

Enter the Additional Medicare Tax your parents paid for 2015 from their 2015 IRS Form 8959, line 18. Enter 0 if Form 8959 was not filed. PI-142A

Enter the amount of 2015 education credits (American Opportunity, Hope and Lifetime Learning) that your parents claimed on their 2015 IRS Form 1040, line 50. PI-145A

Enter the amount of your parents' itemized deductions for 2015 from their 2015 IRS Schedule A, line 29. Enter "0" (zero) if they did not itemize deductions. PI-150A

Enter the income parent 1 earned from work in 2015 from his or her 2015 IRS Form 1040, lines 7, 12, and 18 and IRS Schedule K-1 (Form 1065), Box 14 (Code A). If lines 12 or 18 or box 14 are negative, treat them as zero. If your parents filed a joint return, enter only parent 1's portion of lines 7, 12, and 18 and K-1, box 14. (Parent 1 is the parent you entered in PD-105.) PI-155A

Enter the income parent 2 earned or expects to earn from work in 2015 from his or her 2015 IRS Form 1040, lines 7, 12, and 18 and IRS Schedule K-1 (Form 1065), Box 14 (Code A). If lines 12 or 18 or Box 14 are negative, treat them as zero. If your parents filed a joint return, enter only parent 2's portion of lines 7, 12, and 18 and K-1, box 14. (Parent 2 is the parent you entered in PD-195.)

PI-160A

Commissioned officers only - Enter the combat pay or special combat pay that your parents received for 2015 that was **taxable and included in your parents' adjusted gross income (AGI)** because one or both of them are commissioned officers. It is usually a portion of the amount reported in his or her W-2 Box 1. Do not enter untaxed combat pay reported in W-2 Box 12, Code Q. This does not apply to commissioned warrant officers.

PI-163A

Enter the untaxed social security benefits your parents received or expect to receive for all family members **except you**, the student, in 2015.

PI-165A

Enter the amount of Temporary Assistance for Needy Families (TANF) your parents received or expect to receive in 2015.

PI-175

Enter the amount of child support your parents **received or expect to receive** for all children in 2015. (Do not enter the amount of child support they paid or expect to pay. Enter that amount in PE-100.)

PI-180A

Enter the amount of deductible IRA and/or SEP, SIMPLE, or Keogh **payments** your parents made in 2015 as reported on their 2015 IRS Form 1040, lines 28 and 32.

PI-185A

Enter the untaxed portions of IRA distributions, excluding "rollovers," your parents **received** in 2015. These are reported on 2015 IRS Form 1040, lines 15a minus 15b.

PI-187A

Enter the amount of **payments** (paid directly or withheld from earnings) to tax-deferred pension and savings plans your parents made or expect to make in 2015 including, but not limited to, amounts reported on W-2 Forms in Boxes 12a through 12d, codes D, E, F, G, H, and S. Include untaxed payments to 401(k) and 403(b) plans.

PI-190A

Enter the untaxed portion of pensions, excluding "rollovers," your parents **received** in 2015. These are reported on 2015 IRS Form 1040, lines 16a minus 16b.

PI-192A

Enter the amount of the tuition and fees deduction your parents claimed on their 2015 IRS Form 1040 line 34.

PI-195A

Enter the total amount withheld from your parents' wages in 2015 to contribute to a flexible spending account for medical expenses.

PI-200A

Enter the total amount withheld from your parents' wages in 2015 to contribute to a flexible spending account for dependent care expenses.

PI-201A

Enter the amount of the health savings account deduction your parents claimed on their 2015 IRS Form 1040 line 25.

PI-202A

Enter the total amount withheld from your parents' wages in 2015 to contribute to a Health Savings Account (HSA).

PI-203A

Enter the amount of Earned Income Credit your parents claimed on their 2015 IRS Form 1040, line 66a.

PI-205A

Enter the additional child tax credit your parents claimed on their 2015 IRS Form 1040, line 67.

PI-207A

Enter the amount of housing, food, and other living allowances your parents received or expect to receive in 2015 from their employer or other sources as members of the military, clergy, or other profession. Include cash payments and cash value of benefits. Don't include the value of on-base military housing or the value of a basic military allowance for housing.

PI-210A

Enter the value of on-base military housing or the value of the basic military allowance for housing your parents received or expect to receive in 2015 as members of the military. Include cash payments and cash value of benefits.

PI-211A

Enter the value of veterans' non-educational benefits such as Disability, Death Pension, or Dependency & Indemnity Compensation (DIC) or VA Educational Work-Study allowances your parents received or expect to receive in 2015.

PI-212A

Enter the amount of tax-exempt interest income your parents received in 2015 as reported on their 2015 IRS Form 1040, line 8b.

PI-215A

Enter the amount of foreign income exclusion your parents reported on their 2015 IRS Form 2555, line 45 or Form 2555EZ, line 18.

PI-220A

Enter the amount of cash your parents received and any money paid on their behalf (e.g., bills) in 2015. (Don't include child support or any other amounts reported elsewhere on this application.)

PI-230A

Enter the amount of other untaxed income your parents received in 2015. See the worksheet for types of income to include and the instructions for types of income to exclude. Worksheet

PI-225A

CollegeBoard.com

PROFILE Online 2016-17

HELP DESK | CONTACT US | LOG OUT OF PROFILE

SEARCH

APPLICATION

Back to Registration | Back to Home Page | Add/Remove Colleges | Previous | Save & Continue

SAVE | SAVE & EXIT | SUBMIT | PRINT/REVIEW APPLICATION

GO TO SECTION: Select Section

STATUS: APPLICATION NOT SUBMITTED

Parents' 2014 Income & Benefits (PP)

This section asks for information about the student's parents' income and benefits from the previous year. Any time a question says "you" or "your" it is referring to the student. Any time a question says "parents" it is referring to the student's parent(s) whose information is being given on this application. If a question does not apply, enter "0" (zero).

Help Code

Enter your parents' 2014 adjusted gross income from their 2014 IRS Form 1040, line 37.

PP-100A

Enter the income tax your parents paid for 2014 from their 2014 IRS Form 1040, line 56.

PP-105A

Enter the amount of your parents' itemized deductions for 2014 from their 2014 IRS Schedule A, line 29. Enter "0" (zero) if they did not itemize deductions.

PP-110

Enter the amount of your parents' 2014 untaxed income and benefits. Worksheet

PP-115A

SAVE | SAVE & EXIT | SUBMIT | PRINT/REVIEW APPLICATION

Back to Registration | Back to Home Page | Add/Remove Colleges | Previous | Save & Continue

---

CollegeBoard.com

PROFILE Online 2016-17

HELP DESK | CONTACT US | LOG OUT OF PROFILE

SEARCH

APPLICATION

Back to Registration | Back to Home Page | Add/Remove Colleges | Previous | Save & Continue

SAVE | SAVE & EXIT | SUBMIT | PRINT/REVIEW APPLICATION

GO TO SECTION: Select Section

STATUS: APPLICATION NOT SUBMITTED

Parents' 2016 Expected Income & Benefits (PF)

This section asks for information about the student's parents' expected income and benefits. Any time a question says "you" or "your" it is referring to the student. Any time a question says "parents" it is referring to the student's parent(s) whose information is being given on this application. If a question does not apply, enter "0" (zero). If the expected total income and benefits will differ from the 2015 total by 10% or more, explain in Section ES.

Help Code

Enter the amount of income parent 1 expects to earn from work in 2016. (Parent 1 is the parent you entered in PD-105.)

PF-100A

Enter the amount of income parent 2 expects to earn from work in 2016. (Parent 2 is the parent you entered in PD-195.)

PF-105A

Enter the amount of other taxable income and benefits your parents expect to receive in 2016.

PF-110A

Enter the amount of untaxed income and benefits your parents expect to receive in 2016. Worksheet

PF-115A

SAVE | SAVE & EXIT | SUBMIT | PRINT/REVIEW APPLICATION

Back to Registration | Back to Home Page | Add/Remove Colleges | Previous | Save & Continue

CollegeBoard.com

PROFILE Online 2016-17

HELP DESK   CONTACT US   LOG OUT OF PROFILE

SEARCH

APPLICATION

Back to Registration   Back to Home Page   Add/Remove Colleges   Previous   Save & Continue

SAVE   SAVE & EXIT   SUBMIT   PRINT/REVIEW APPLICATION

GO TO SECTION: Select Section

STATUS: APPLICATION NOT SUBMITTED

Parents' Assets (PA)

This section asks for information about the student's parents' assets. Any time a question says "you" or "your" it is referring to the student. Any time a question says "parents" it is referring to the student's parent(s) whose information is being given on this application. If a numeric question does not apply, enter "0" (zero). If a non-numeric question (e.g. yes/no questions about asset ownership) does not apply, you may leave it blank.

Help Code

[?] Enter the amount your parents have in their cash, savings, and checking accounts as of today.   PA-100A

[?] Enter the total value of **your parents'** assets held in the names of your (the student's) brothers and sisters who are under age 19 and not college students.   PA-105A

[?] What is the total current market value of your parents' investments? Do not include your parents' home, business, farm, real estate, or retirement plans. Worksheet   PA-120A

[?] What do your parents owe on their investments?   PA-125A

[?] What is the current market value of your parents' home?   PA-130A

[?] What do your parents owe on their home?   PA-135A

[?] What year was your parents' home purchased?   --Select an answer--   PA-140

[?] What was the purchase price of your parents' home?   PA-145A

[?] What is the total current market value of your parents' real estate other than their home?   PA-180A

[?] What do your parents owe on other real estate they own?   PA-185A

[?] What year was your parents' other real estate purchased?   --Select an answer--   PA-190A

[?] What was the purchase price of your parents' other real estate?   PA-195A

SAVE   SAVE & EXIT   SUBMIT   PRINT/REVIEW APPLICATION

Back to Registration   Back to Home Page   Add/Remove Colleges   Previous   Save & Continue

CollegeBoard.com

PROFILE Online 2016–17

HELP DESK | CONTACT US | LOG OUT OF PROFILE

SEARCH

APPLICATION

Back to Registration | Back to Home Page | Add/Remove Colleges | Previous | Save & Continue
SAVE | SAVE & EXIT | SUBMIT | PRINT/REVIEW APPLICATION

GO TO SECTION: Select Section

STATUS: APPLICATION NOT SUBMITTED

Parents' Expenses (PE)

This section asks for information about the student's parents' expenses. Any time a question says "you" or "your" it is referring to the student. Any time a question says "parents" it is referring to the student's parent(s) whose information is being given on this application. If a question does not apply, answer "0" (zero).

Help Code

Enter the amount of child support your parent(s) **paid or expect to pay** in 2015 because of divorce or separation or as the result of a legal requirement. (Do not enter the amount of child support you received or expect to receive. Enter that amount in PI-180.) — PE-100

Enter the amount of child support your parent(s) **expect to pay** in 2016 because of divorce or separation or as the result of a legal requirement. (Do not enter the amount of child support you expect to receive.) — PE-105

Enter how much your parent(s) repaid or expect to repay on their educational loans in 2015. — PE-110

Enter how much your parent(s) expect to repay on their educational loans in 2016. — PE-115

Enter the amount of medical and dental expenses your parent(s) paid or expect to pay in 2015 that were not covered by insurance or a medical or dental plan. — PE-120A

Enter the amount of medical and dental expenses your parent(s) expect to pay in 2016 that will not be covered by insurance or a medical or dental plan. — PE-125

Enter the total elementary, junior high school, and high school **tuition** your parent(s) paid or expect to pay for dependent children in 2015. Do not include tuition paid for you, the student. — PE-130A

Enter the total elementary, junior high school, and high school **tuition** your parent(s) expect to pay for dependent children in 2016. Do not include tuition paid for you, the student. — PE-135

For how many dependent children did your parent(s) pay elementary, junior high school, and high school tuition for in 2015? Do not include you, the student. — PE-140A

For how many dependent children do your parent(s) expect to pay elementary, junior high school, and high school tuition for in 2016? Do not include you, the student. — PE-145

What is your parents' monthly home mortgage payment? (If none, explain in Explanations/Special Circumstances (ES).) — PE-150A

SAVE | SAVE & EXIT | SUBMIT | PRINT/REVIEW APPLICATION
Back to Registration | Back to Home Page | Add/Remove Colleges | Previous | Save & Continue

Then you are asked about your information, income, assets, benefits, and expenses.

CollegeBoard.com

PROFILE Online 2016-17

SEARCH

APPLICATION

| Back to Registration | Back to Home Page | Add/Remove Colleges | | Previous | Save & Continue |
| SAVE | SAVE & EXIT | | SUBMIT | PRINT/REVIEW APPLICATION |

GO TO SECTION: Select Section

STATUS: APPLICATION NOT SUBMITTED

Student's Data (SD)

This section asks for information about the student. Any time a question says "you" or "your" it is referring to the student. If a financial question does not apply, enter "0" (zero). If a non-financial question (e.g. name of school) does not apply, you may leave it blank.

Help Code

Enter the name of the school, college, or university you attend/attended during the 2015-16 academic year.		SD-100
What is/was your year in school during the 2015-16 school year?	--Select an answer--	SD-105A
How much did you or will you receive in scholarships, grants, and gift aid during the 2015-16 academic year?		SD-110A
How much did or will your parents pay for your education for the 2015-16 academic year?		SD-115A
What is your state, territory, or province of legal residence?	--Select an answer--	SD-120
When you were age 13 or older, were both of your parents deceased, were you in foster care, or were you a dependent/ward of the court?	--Select an answer--	SD-145
At any time on or after July 1, 2015 did you receive an official determination that you are an unaccompanied youth who is homeless or at risk of being homeless?	--Select an answer--	SD-150
Are you, or have you been, an Upward Bound participant?	--Select an answer--	SD-159

| SAVE | SAVE & EXIT | | SUBMIT | PRINT/REVIEW APPLICATION |
| Back to Registration | Back to Home Page | Add/Remove Colleges | | Previous | Save & Continue |

CollegeBoard.com

PROFILE Online 2016-17

SEARCH

APPLICATION

| Back to Registration | Back to Home Page | Add/Remove Colleges | | Previous | Save & Continue |
| SAVE | SAVE & EXIT | | SUBMIT | PRINT/REVIEW APPLICATION |

GO TO SECTION: Select Section

STATUS: APPLICATION NOT SUBMITTED

Student's 2015 Income and Benefits (SI)

This section asks for information about the student's (and the student's spouse's, if married) income and benefits. Any time a question says "you" or "your" it is referring to the student (and student's spouse's, if married). If a question does not apply, enter "0" (zero).

Help Code

Enter the income you earned or expect to earn from work in 2015.		SI-125G
Enter the amount of taxable dividend and interest income you earned or expect to earn in 2015.		SI-135B
Enter the amount of any other untaxed income you received or expect to receive in 2015. Worksheet		SI-160G
Enter the amount of 2015 AmeriCorps earnings you reported or expect to report to the IRS in your adjusted gross income.		SI-165B

| SAVE | SAVE & EXIT | | SUBMIT | PRINT/REVIEW APPLICATION |
| Back to Registration | Back to Home Page | Add/Remove Colleges | | Previous | Save & Continue |

CollegeBoard.com

PROFILE Online 2016-17

HELP DESK   CONTACT US   LOG OUT OF PROFILE

SEARCH

APPLICATION

Back to Registration   Back to Home Page   Add/Remove Colleges   Previous   Save & Continue

SAVE   SAVE & EXIT   SUBMIT   PRINT/REVIEW APPLICATION

GO TO SECTION: Select Section   STATUS: APPLICATION NOT SUBMITTED

Student's Expected Resources for 2016-17 (SR)

This section asks for information about the student (and the student's spouse's, if married) expected income and resources. Any time a question says "you" or "your" it is referring to the student. If a question does not apply, enter "0" (zero).

Help Code

If you received/will receive veterans' education benefits during July 1, 2016 - June 30, 2017, what type of benefits did you/will you receive?

--Select an answer--   SR-100

Enter the amount of veterans' education benefits you received/expect to receive per month during July 1, 2016 - June 30, 2017.   SR-103

For how many months did you/will you receive veterans' education benefits during July 1, 2016 - June 30, 2017?   SR-105

Enter the total amount you expect to earn in wages, salaries, tips, etc. during the summer of 2016. (3 months)   SR-110A

Enter the total amount you expect to earn in wages, salaries, tips, etc. during the 2016-17 school year. (9 months)   SR-115

Enter the total amount of grants, scholarships, fellowships, etc. including AmeriCorps benefits you received or expect to receive from sources other than the colleges or universities to which you are applying. (List sources in Explanations/Special Circumstances (ES).)   SR-150

Enter the amount of tuition benefits you will receive from your parents' employer(s) and/or your employer.   SR-155A

Enter the amount your parents think they will be able to pay for your 2016-17 college expenses.   SR-160A

Enter the total amount you expect to receive from your relatives and all other sources. (List sources and amounts in Explanations/Special Circumstances (ES).)   SR-165A

SAVE   SAVE & EXIT   SUBMIT   PRINT/REVIEW APPLICATION

Back to Registration   Back to Home Page   Add/Remove Colleges   Previous   Save & Continue

CollegeBoard.com

PROFILE Online 2016-17

HELP DESK   CONTACT US   LOG OUT OF PROFILE

SEARCH

APPLICATION

Back to Registration   Back to Home Page   Add/Remove Colleges   Previous   Save & Continue

SAVE   SAVE & EXIT   SUBMIT   PRINT/REVIEW APPLICATION

GO TO SECTION: Select Section   STATUS: APPLICATION NOT SUBMITTED

Student's Assets (SA)

This section asks for information about the student's (and student's spouse's, if married) assets. Any time a question says "you" or "your" it is referring to the student (and student's spouse's, if married). If a numeric financial question does not apply, enter "0" (zero). If a non-financial question (e.g. yes/no questions about an asset you do not own) does not apply, you may leave it blank.

Help Code

[?] Enter the amount you have in cash, savings, and checking accounts as of today.   SA-100A

[?] Enter the total value of your non-education IRA, Keogh, 401k, 403b, etc. accounts as of December 31, 2015.   SA-105

[?] What is the total current market value of your investments including Uniform Gifts to Minors? Worksheet   SA-110A

[?] What do you owe on your investments?   SA-115A

[?] Enter the total value of all of the trusts of which you are a beneficiary. If you do not or will not benefit from a trust, enter zero (0) and skip the next two questions (SA-175 and SA-180).   SA-170A

[?] If you are the beneficiary of a trust, is any income or part of the principal from the trust(s) currently available?   --Select an answer--   SA-175

[?] If you are the beneficiary of a trust, who established the trust?   --Select an answer--   SA-180

SAVE   SAVE & EXIT   SUBMIT   PRINT/REVIEW APPLICATION

Back to Registration   Back to Home Page   Add/Remove Colleges   Previous   Save & Continue

In the last screen, you get to explain any special circumstances or unusual expenses you have that might affect the calculation of your expected family contribution.

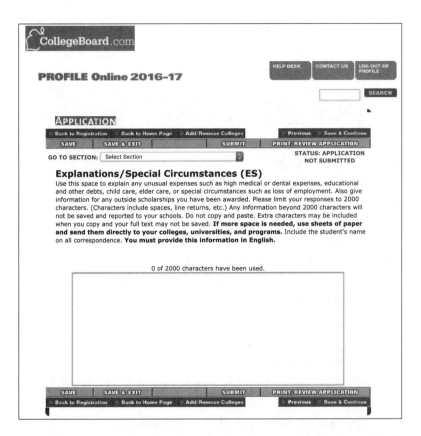

Once you have completed the CSS PROFILE, you will receive an electronic acknowledgement, just as you do from the FAFSA. The acknowledgement will show the data you provided, including the colleges you want to receive your information. You have a pay a small sum as an application fee and an additional amount for each college you specify. If you need a fee waiver, there is a process set up to help you.

For more information about the CSS PROFILE, you can go to https://student.collegeboard.org/css-financial-aid-profile.

Once your application is submitted and accepted, and the data are analyzed and sent to the colleges you specified, communication will be between you and the colleges themselves. If you need to send the information to additional colleges, you can do so by logging back in to The College Board PROFILE site.

🎓 Timing

The rules for applying for financial aid have changed, effective October 1, 2016.

For federal financial aid, for which you use the FAFSA, you will be able to apply beginning October 1 of the year preceding fall enrollment. That is new for 2016. You can also complete the CSS PROFILE as early as October 1.

For enrollment in fall 2017, this means you can begin the application process October 1, 2016. Because there will be two possible years for which the financial aid applications can be used (i.e., students enrolling in spring 2016 can still apply for federal aid), make certain that you are completing the correct application.

You do not have to apply immediately on October 1. The reason for that early date is simply that it ties into the admission application timing. But deadlines for aid are not until February or March at the earliest. Still, it doesn't hurt to get your applications in early, especially if you are applying for early admission.

Note, also, that both the FAFSA and PROFILE will ask you about the prior-prior year income—that is, for enrollment beginning in fall 2017, you qualify based on income from the 2015 year. That is a change from previous applications. What that means is that you will not have to use estimated income and you can more than likely use the IRS data retrieval tool, since your income taxes will have been filed months before (due April 2016).

Pay careful attention to the instructions in each application so you don't use the wrong year to report income. Assets are always reported as of the date you complete the application.

Again, if you have any questions or concerns, you can call 1-800-4-FED-AID (about the federal process and FAFSA) and 866-630-9305 (for questions about the PROFILE).

🎓 Additional Information

Often colleges will ask for additional information or documentation for what you reported on the FAFSA and/or PRO-FILE. This is strictly up to the college itself, not the federal government or the application processor, although sometimes your application is "flagged" for verification by the government.

Since most applicants will be able to provide income information directly from the IRS (again, under the new rules the base year is the prior-prior year), there are other sources of income that may be questioned, such as nontaxable income or assets.

If you are asked for any documentation or additional information, you should make it a point to respond as quickly as possible. A delay in sending requested information could mean you don't get your award in time or that you don't get the full amount. Remember that there are many other students applying, and whereas there is no limit to the amount of Pell Grant available, there is a limited amount of grant aid that the college itself controls, especially its own money. There are also deadlines that the college has established, and state grant agencies also limit the funds they provide to students who apply by a specific date.

If you are concerned that you may not be able to get the information to the college on a timely basis, call or write and explain the reason. If it's reasonable, the college will likely do what it can to accommodate the special circumstance.

Once all your information is in and, for most incoming first year students, you have been accepted for enrollment, the financial aid office will send out an "award" letter detailing all the aid the college is offering. The award letter will show not only the specific dollar amounts awarded but also the college budget and calculated expected family contribution they used to base the award. Some colleges will alter that calculation based on policies they have. For example, some colleges will add back into the total income any "second business" losses or real estate depreciation. Not to defend these colleges, but many professionals believe that the limited dollars available should go to the neediest students, not necessarily to those whose parents have income offset by tax losses. There is generally very little you can do about it other than appeal, but just know that some colleges do this.

In the next chapter, we'll go further into the financial aid awards (referred to as "packages").

CHAPTER 5

How Much Will We Get?

Making Your College Choice

Ideally the financial aid award will cover the entire amount you need to pay for college. Unfortunately, this isn't the case in most colleges.

Packaging and Need

Once you've completed the application process, the next step will usually be up to the colleges. If the colleges have requested additional information, documentation, or an explanation, be certain that you supply it as soon as you can. You don't want to miss out on any potential grant aid just because you didn't get back to the college on a timely basis.

But assuming the schools have all they need from you, they will go through their procedures and send you an award letter. As stated earlier, this letter will show you the budget, the expected family contribution used to determine your financial need, and a detail of the specific financial aid awards the school is offering. This is referred to as the "package" since, for most students, it is a combination of several different types of assistance. Also, for most students at most colleges, there is an amount left over that doesn't fully meet

the total cost of the college expenses. Most colleges are not
in a position to fully fund all the students' financial need, so
they leave a "gap." This portion is, essentially, an amount you
and your family will have to come up with that the college
cannot supply.

Some colleges, especially those with the largest endow-
ments (i.e., the most competitive colleges such as the Ivies),
will award the full need.

The following are sample awards taken from individual
college websites. The awards were derived by using the college's own net price calculator. The hypothetical family we
used to determine the EFC is based on the following:

1. Two-parent family; older parent is forty-seven
   years old.
2. Student is seventeen and attending college for the
   first time.
3. Student and parents are in-state residents where
   the colleges are located.
4. Total income is $90,000 all in wages (one parent
   earns $60,000, the other $30,000). No other income.
5. Parents have $30,000 in assets.
6. Home value is $360,000 with $240,000 in outstanding mortgage.
7. Student has $1,000 income and no assets.
8. Calculated expected family contribution (EFC) is
   $12,127 (federal methodology; FM) and $13,036 (institutional methodology; IM), which includes $1,900
   in "student contribution."

Sample Packages

We gathered several sample packages from actual colleges
using the college's own net price calculator. The colleges selected represent a private four-year university and a flagship
public four-year university, both in-state and out-of-state, a

nonflagship public state college, and a community college. Since the private and flagship public universities require their students to submit the PROFILE, we have used the IM expected family contribution, including the student contribution. For the public state college, we used the FM-calculated EFC, which, as you see above, is about $900 less. In order to keep costs consistent, we used the on-campus living option except for the community college, for which we used the "not living with parents" option.

Following are two tables, the first one showing the costs at each of the types of colleges listed, and the second showing the sample packages awarded to our fictional student and his family.

Table 5.1: Comparison of College Costs at Private Four-Year, Public Four-Year, and Community Colleges

Costs	Private four-year	Flagship public four-year (in-state)	Flagship public four-year (out-of-state)	Public state college (in-state)	Community college
Tuition/fees	$48,450	$19,400	$41,100	$9,900	$1,400
Room/board	$14,520	$10,980	$10,980	$10,730	$12,050
Books/supplies	$1,200	$1,300	$1,300	$1,000	$1,500
Transportation	$630	$525	$925	–	–
Personal	$1,320	$1,450	$1,450	$3,550	$4,100
Total cost	$66,120	$33,655	$55,755	$25,180	$19,050

Table 5.2: Comparison of Financial Aid Packages at Private

| Four-Year, Public Four-Year, and Community Colleges | | | | |
	Private four-year	Flagship public four-year (in-state)	Flagship public four-year (out-of-state)	Public state college (in-state)	Community college
Inst. grant	$50,850	$14,520	$14,000	$1,700	$500
Total grant	$50,850	$14,520	$14,000	$1,700	$500
Est. net price	$15,270	$19,135	$41,755	$23,480	$18,550
Student loan	$6,700	$4,500	$5,500	$3,500	$3,500
Student work	$2,000	$1,900	$1,900	–	–
EFC	$13,036 (IM)	$13,036 (IM)	$13,036 (IM)	$12,127 (FM)	$12,127 (FM)
Unmet need	$ 6,570	$12,735	$34,355	$19,980	$15,050
Total out-of-pocket cost	$15,270	$19,135	$41,755	$23,480	$18,550

The bottom line shows that the lowest out-of-pocket cost to this particular family is at the private four-year college. This result is not at all surprising to me; as you recall, I made this point in the opening remarks of this book. Private colleges have a great deal more available money that they can spend on students to enable them to attend. Public flagship colleges also have their own discretionary money, but most state colleges and community colleges have almost none of their own scholarship or grant money to give to students to help defray the costs. That explains that, while the "sticker price" of the private four-year college in our sample is almost $66,000 as compared to the sticker price of the community college, which is only $19,000, the family of the student attending the private four-year college will spend almost $4,000 less per year.

Now, to be fair, we have not exactly kept everything constant in our examples. The living expenses at the community college shown are higher than the other colleges. And if the student lives at home, where most community college students live, those living expenses drop dramatically. But the same can be said of the other colleges. Living at home is definitely cheaper than living on campus or in an apartment off campus. Students attending a private college or the state college in their own city can live at home, too.

But the key to reading this table is to look at the bottom line: How much will my family have to spend if I (or my child) go to each of these colleges? You cannot simply look at the sticker price, but you also cannot simply look at the amount of unmet need. Some colleges will include loans and work in the unmet need figure. But you have to consider that loans are just a means of deferring the cost. Ultimately they're still part of your out-of-pocket cost.

The real bottom line that a family has to pay includes all loans and work or, in other words, the total cost minus the total grant. In the examples for the table, at the private four-year college, the family will be responsible for $15,056; at the in-state flagship public college, the family will shell out $19,108; at a flagship public college in another state, this family will pay $41,725; at an in-state public college (not the flagship), the family will pay $23,492; and at the local community college (assuming the student does not live at home), the family will pay $18,795.

So what's the best choice for this family?

The beauty of this illustration is that this example is not very different from sample packages for many families with many colleges. I can tell you honestly that when I selected the colleges to use in these tables, I did not know what the results would be. I admit that I changed the private four-year selection, but I did so because I knew that the college I had originally selected would be considered more highly selective and does not award any merit aid (most of the highly selective colleges do not award merit aid). I wanted to show an example of a private college that was more representative of the colleges in this country. And many private colleges do award merit aid in combination with need-based aid.

There are several things I find most surprising. One is that there is only a $4,000 difference in the out-of-pocket cost to the family between the private four-year and the flagship public four-year, despite the huge difference in sticker price. Equally surprising is the fact that the out-of-pocket cost to the family at the state college, supposedly the less expensive college because of the state support, is actually considerably higher than both the private and flagship public.

Just to summarize, and in the spirit of the title of this book, the total loan awarded by each of the colleges in the sample are:

Private four-year: $6,700
Flagship public: $4,500
State college: $3,500
Community college: $3,500

However, the unmet need (including the EFC) for each college is:

Private four-year: $6,570
Flagship public: $12,735
State college: $19,980
Community college: $15,050

How this unmet need is met is the next topic. But when considering the out-of-pocket cost to you and your family, loans should be in the mix since, in actuality, you are paying the loans—you're just paying for them over time.

Meeting Your Share of Expenses

Throughout this book, I have made the point that first and foremost, it is the responsibility of the family to pay for the education of the family members *to the extent they are able.* I emphasize "to the extent they are able" because we know that it not always the case. First off, when students attend a publically supported college, taxpayers are subsidizing the cost. When the children of the richest people in the world go to a public college, the family is not paying the full cost of that education; taxpayers are helping keep the tuition low. They could be paying more but they don't have to. Second, when a student gets a merit scholarship—because of any number of reasons such as athletics, special talent, or high grades—the family is also not paying the full cost. The college itself is subsidizing that student so the family is not paying as much as "they are able." There are other times when the family is not paying as much as they are able, but the point is clear: it's not always fair.

There are ways to help make this "fairer," and the following list enumerates some of those ways:

1. Students who are awarded outside scholarships often do not have to borrow as much. In effect, they are reducing the amount of out-of-pocket cost. So see if your student can qualify for an outside scholarship.

2. Students who are legacy students—that is, their parents attended the college, too—may get more grant aid (also called a "tuition discount") because the family is then more likely to donate, so the college sees value in having that student attend.

3. Students who, for any number of reasons—including where they're from, ethnicity, and specific area of interest—are viewed as "attractive" to a college are given more grant aid or a tuition discount.

4. Students whose parents work for a company that provides educational benefits for dependents get reimbursed for some or all of the costs. Be sure to check if your employer has this benefit.

But if you don't fall into one of those categories, you are stuck with the "to the extent you are able" concept. Often, this is one of the biggest barriers families face—namely, meeting the calculated EFC amount.

Let's explore some of the ways you can do so.

Negotiation

One of the common misconceptions about college financial aid is that colleges will routinely negotiate with families about the amount of aid offered. True, colleges do make changes to award packages, but they do so after reviewing files for errors, when families tell them about unusual expenses, or if the family has a drop in income. So if your family does have a special expense that was unforeseen (health issue), or if your income drops (perhaps because of job loss), explaining the situation to the financial aid office can help. Be prepared to hear "no," but also be prepared to accept the admission offer if the financial aid office says "yes." As you can guess, financial aid administrators have heard just about every story imaginable, so they will be skeptical when a family with a considerably high income starts pleading poverty. But reasonable compromises can be made, especially when the college wants the student to attend. This is true for later years, too. Remember that the college has a big investment in the student continuing to graduation. They can't easily replace students entering the sophomore or junior year. So if your story is compelling, write, call, or visit the financial aid counseling staff and ask about special circumstances. Again, be prepared to hear "no." But be equally prepared to have your child attend there if the financial aid office says "yes."

529 Plans and Financial Aid Consequences

Simply put, and as the IRS states, a 529 plan is "a plan oper-
ated by a state or educational institution, with tax advantages and potentially other incentives to make it easier to
save for college and other postsecondary training for a designated beneficiary, such as a child or grandchild." The money
invested stays in the account until it is used by the beneficiary. The key is that the funds in the account grow tax-free,
and withdrawals of the earnings are not taxed if used for college expenses. They are called 529 plans because that is the
section number of the IRS code. Anyone can set up or contribute to a 529 plan, and there are some tax benefits available to both the recipient and investor.

There are two types of 529 plans. The first is a prepaid
tuition plan that can be set up or administered either by a
state or by an eligible institution of higher education. Under
this plan, you purchase tuition at the institution (or the state
college) based on current tuition rates. When the student
attends, the tuition is paid from the 529 prepaid tuition plan.
Even if the tuition has increased beyond the earnings of the
plan, you are not responsible for paying the higher amount.

The second type of plan is a savings plan very similar to
an IRA in that the investment grows tax-free and withdrawals
are not taxed if used by the beneficiary for college expenses.

Check with your tax advisor about tax consequences, but
note that funds in a 529 plan may be considered in the need
analysis to determine the EFC. If the student is the owner
of the plan, then the funds are considered student assets,
which has a large effect on the EFC. If the funds are in the
parent's name, then they are considered parent assets and, as
such, have a much smaller effect in the need analysis (maximum of 5.6 percent). If the funds are not in either the parent's
or student's name, then they are not reported on the Free
Application for Federal Student Aid (FAFSA). *But*, when distributions are made to the student, those distributions will

be considered income to the student, which will affect the EFC the next time the FAFSA is completed.

As the EDvisors Network suggests, a way to get around some of these consequences is by changing ownership of the account to the student at the proper time—that is, after the FAFSA is filed. For more information, check https://www.edvisors.com/plan-for-college/saving-for-college/529-college-savings-plans/financial-aid.

Outside Scholarships

Another common misconception about college financial aid is that there are millions of dollars in college scholarships that go unclaimed every year. While it is true there is money out there that goes unused, it's not what you think. The XYZ Foundation or the ABC Company, both of which award scholarships to students, do go through all the dollars they have allocated for that year. What does not get fully used is the money set aside for employee benefits, which many companies call "scholarships." Local community groups may award some small scholarships, but only if people apply for them.

That said, and as we discussed in an earlier chapter, students should go through the scholarship search databases available online and apply for any that are appropriate.

Some words of caution, however: First, don't spend more time on the application than it's worth. Most of the large scholarships awarded from foundations and large companies are very, very competitive. Some require extensive research or great essays. If that's in your wheelhouse, great. Go for it. But don't neglect your studies (or other scholarship opportunities) just to apply for something that may be out of your reach. Instead, focus on smaller, local organizations that award scholarships to local students. You may be pleasantly surprised to get several smaller awards of a few hundred dollars from service clubs and local churches and religious groups.

Second, if you receive any need-based financial aid, any outside scholarship you get may reduce the amount of financial aid you receive. Although that sounds unfair, think about it for a minute. Need-based aid is money you need. If your need is met through outside money (scholarships, gifts, your family's assets, etc.), then you don't need the college's money. If the cost of education is $30,000 and the scholarship is $30,000, then you no longer have need, even if your EFC is zero.

However, outside scholarships can and do count toward your EFC and any unmet need. Furthermore, outside scholarships can reduce your self-help aid, not your gift aid. So if you do get a scholarship worth $3,500, and your financial aid package includes a loan of $3,500, you can say no to the loan. But be sure the financial aid office is aware of the outside scholarship.

One last caution that bears repeating: under no circumstance should you ever pay a company to do a scholarship search for you. As I discussed earlier, there are several free scholarship search engines available online. They all use essentially the same database. So never pay for a scholarship search.

Work-Study Versus Outside Jobs

Often the student package will include a Federal Work-Study (FWS) award, generally in the range of a few thousand dollars. Essentially, that is the amount the student can earn during the year.

Work-study jobs are not really too different than any other job. The primary difference is in who pays the worker's salary. With a work-study job, the college, through the money it gets from the federal government for FWS, is paying a portion of the salary, while the employer pays the rest. The worker still has to earn the salary through work, and students must be paid at least minimum wage. Many work-study jobs are on campus. In fact, most college departments depend on work-study students to fill the labor pool. They are essentially getting a worker for sometimes as low as forty cents on the dollar. So they can hire more students to get their work done. One of the perks of being in charge of the Federal Work-Study program was our opportunity to find the best and brightest students to work in the financial aid office. They were essential workers, as any financial aid administrator will attest, and financial aid offices couldn't run without them. It usually worked out well for the work-study students, too, since they were always up on all the regulations surrounding financial aid (and it was often very rewarding work for the students).

On-campus jobs are also highly desirable from the student's point of view for several reasons:

1. On-campus jobs are all about convenience. You can easily put in few hours' work in between classes or before/after your classes for the day. There is no commute time, so you are making as much as you possibly can.

2. You can sometimes find a good work-study job in the department you are majoring in. That gives you access to professors and other students in the department. Even if you are doing menial work in the department office, you can still interact and form relationships with your professors. That could prove invaluable in future opportunities and graduate school recommendations.

3. On-campus employers are generally very amenable to your changing schedule. And most will bend over backward to make sure you have the time you need to study for a big test or get a paper in.

4. On-campus employers also generally do not require that you work during school breaks. That allows you to go home or take advantage of other opportunities.

All that said, if you already have a job that you like, is convenient, and pays you more than what you can earn through the FWS program, by all means, keep it. Most FWS jobs pay close to minimum wage. If your wages are significantly higher, you should seriously consider keeping your current job as long as your employer allows you some flexibility around your class and test schedule.

If you do maintain your own job, decline the FWS portion of your award and be sure to let the financial aid office know that you have your own job. You'll have to report your earnings the next time you apply for aid (every year), so you'll want to make sure you don't earn so much you lose your eligibility for other financial aid.

Living Above Your Means

By design, student budgets are barebones, providing just as much as you need to get by. Some of the costs are fixed—in particular, tuition and fees and on-campus room and board. The rest of the budget is an estimate. Colleges commission studies to determine the real costs of being a student, but a budget of, say, $1400 for books and supplies is clearly an average. An art student will clearly spend more than that. On the other hand, a literature course might only require a handful of books, none of which fall into the realm of expensive textbooks. The same can be said of all the other indirect costs such as transportation and, everyone's favorite, "personal" expenses. When devising these budgets, we used to say that even students on financial aid can have some fun, so we always built in something for those late-night pizzas or going out once in a while to a movie.

So while the budgets used are fairly low, they are generally pretty realistic. Students really can make it though a year on what the budget says, even though it doesn't seem possible. The challenge you will have is not only making sure you don't live above your means but also budgeting for the entire year. Very few people can manage to spread out their money for four or five months when they get most of it at the very beginning.

Your task will be to spend your money wisely and to not live above your means. If you're the type who can create spreadsheets to help you, do so. If you're not comfortable living that way, do what you can to keep very close tabs on your spending. And whenever there's a purchase coming up, be very cognizant of the impact it will have on the rest of your semester.

Living Below Your Means

Given the limited amount of money we used to award when I was director of financial aid, I was always wondering how students survived. We were sure they were living under a bridge somewhere. We knew there was an underground economy; otherwise, there was no way people could survive on what we provided. We always tried to make it clear that students should come to us if they were having money troubles and not wait until they were really desperate. We offered small loans and made many phone calls to landlords and creditors on students' behalf, explaining that the student would be receiving financial aid funds that would cover the debt.

The fact is, that's not the best way to do well in college. We knew that, but given the limited amount of money we had available, we couldn't do much more.

Surviving on ramen is a time-honored tradition for college students. But going hungry for days is not. Being a few days late to pay your bills periodically is also common. But getting thrown out of your apartment or having your electricity turned off because you didn't have the money to pay will pretty much ensure that you do poorly in school. It demonstrates that you have a much more serious problem than poor study habits or a few setbacks. It indicates that unless things change, you will very likely drop out or be thrown out of school.

That is the very last thing the college wants. Remember that the college has invested a great deal in you. They want you to succeed. They want you to become an alum. They look forward to you being very successful and contributing to the college later on. They know you're smart enough to succeed and they accepted you into the program.

So just as money should not be the deciding factor in determining which college you should attend, money should not be the key reason for you to fail or drop out. Despite all the bureaucratic barriers and obstacles involved with financial aid, the staff offers an important service, and they are committed to helping you succeed.

Don't wait until you are in a desperate situation before reaching out to the professionals in the financial aid office. They may not always be able to help, but most of the time they can work with you to find the best solution. At the very least, they will know who or what organization might be able to help.

Loans

And finally, we come to using loans to help pay for your education. As I stated right up front in this book, I believe that for many students and families, borrowing to pay for your education is perfectly reasonable and appropriate. An education is a long-term investment and a loan is nothing more than a way to pay for that investment over time. I compared paying for college with buying a house, another long-term investment. No one believes it is wrong to take out a mortgage to pay for your home. A student loan is not very different.

But just as you would shop around for the best mortgage and would research all that's involved, you should also know as much as you can about the loan options you have. In the next chapter, we will explore the terms of student and education loans. We'll also talk about an appropriate amount to borrow so that you don't find yourself in a situation where you are forced to forego key things in order to pay your student loans. And we'll talk also about how much parents should borrow.

Among the considerations is your chosen field of study and also whether your plans would include graduate school. Most financial aid for graduate school is in the form of loan. In your deliberations about borrowing, consider whether you will need to go on to an advanced degree.

And of course, you'll have to think about what alternatives you have to borrowing that allow you to still attend the college of your choice.

Moving Forward to Later Years—Bait and Switch?

One thing that we haven't yet discussed but that comes into play after the freshman year is what happens later on. First, note that students have to reapply for financial aid every year. That means applying between October and February of the freshman year. Make certain you put a reminder on the family calendar! During the Christmas break is a perfect time. The base year will not be the current year but the one for which you filed your tax return the previous April; fortunately, that means you'll have all the data you need. And don't wait too long, since there are likely some deadlines for institutional and state aid that could be as early as February. When everyone is home during the holidays, you can gather around the computer to complete the FAFSA.

You need to know that colleges treat continuing students differently than incoming ones. First of all, the deadline might be later. Second, the award letter might arrive later, though hopefully not too much later, because families will need time to prepare. Third, and perhaps most important, the packaging guidelines will likely be different.

How different will depend on the college. But at a minimum, the college is likely to award sophomores, juniors, and seniors more money in the form of loans. There are a few reasons for this tactic—some with good motivation behind it, some that might rub you the wrong way.

First, under federal regulations, sophomores have higher loan limits than freshman (and juniors and seniors even higher limits). Freshmen can borrow up to $3,500 in subsidized loans and up to $5,500 in a combination of subsidized and unsubsidized loans. Sophomores can borrow an additional $1,000 or up to $4,500 in subsidized loans and a combined total of $6,500 (add another $1,000 for the junior or senior years).

Second, the costs will likely increase in later years. That means, of course, that the college will very likely award the higher loan amount to continuing students, and partially because they can. Even if the cost of education didn't go up, they will likely award the additional $1,000 in loan and, in most instances, take it from the grant aid they awarded.

Does this sound like bait and switch? Well, perhaps. But there is actually sound reasoning behind the decision. The higher amount is because students with two years of education are more likely to get better jobs—higher-paying jobs—over their lifetime than students who have completed just one year of college. You have to admit that it does make sense, just as a student who gets a degree is more likely to earn more in his or her lifetime than someone who doesn't.

Naturally, though, there are many who look at this as "bait and switch"—that is, I got you, I lured you in, and now I'm changing the rules. There's probably a degree of truth that some colleges award more loan to upperclassmen for that reason. And the sad part is that colleges don't really have to announce what they plan to do in later years. There are some colleges that promise no or minimum amounts of loan for students, particularly low-income students. But many colleges do not address the issue in any published material. Since your student is already attending, it would be a simple matter for him or her to pay a visit to the financial aid office and make that inquiry. Many colleges will share their pack-aging guidelines, but may not—and almost never—publish them on their websites.

There's not much you can do about the packaging guide-line changes. You can appeal, and the student might be able to increase the Federal Work-Study award instead of more loan. But it's unlikely the student will get more grant money.

You can try to get an outside scholarship. Having com-pleted one year of college, the student may be better qual-ified and better able to complete a scholarship application. And if awarded, the student may be able to have the loan replaced, not any of the grant award.

Third, the student might be able to get a higher-paying summer (or school-year) job and thus be able to refuse some of the loan and rely on savings and increased earnings.

Beyond that, however, it may be a "grin and bear it" approach, knowing that with additional schooling, the stu-dent will be in a better position to repay the loan.

CHAPTER 6

Paying It Back

About 61% of students who earned bachelor's degrees in 2013–14 from the public and private non-profit four-year institutions . . . borrowed an average of $26,900.

"Trends in Student Aid 2015," The College Board

Two people looking at the numbers above will view them totally differently. For some, 61 percent is a pretty high figure, saying, essentially, well over half of students graduate with debt. And owing $27,000? Wow, that's a lot of money.

Others might have the opposite reaction: Only 61 percent borrow? And only $27,000? That's about the average size of a loan taken out for a new car. Surely that's not something to worry about. You'll be earning so much more by getting your degree, a couple hundred per month is not such a big deal.

Both views are right, of course. For someone who has never made or doesn't know anyone who makes $27,000 a year (obviously including most students and many recent graduates), that's overwhelming. Paying a couple hundred per month is definitely going to affect their lives.

In this book, I can't change your perspective. But I can address the issues surrounding the numbers and, hopefully, make the numbers less onerous.

Commitment

Taking out a loan means making a commitment. But it's not simply a commitment to pay back the money. That's just one part of it. The commitment is in knowing all your rights and responsibilities. If you borrow a few bucks from your friend, you know you owe those few bucks. And there's usually an understanding about when you'll pay it back. You might have said, "I'll pay you back next week after I get paid." And if you can't pay it back then, you'll probably tell your friend that fact. You probably won't blow off your friend.

You may also forget about the loan, especially if it's just a few bucks. That's pretty common. But at one point, either you or your friend will remember (or your friend will finally confront you) and you'll make another commitment to paying it back. This time, you'll probably be a bit more definite about when you'll pay it back. And chances are, you'll make a strong effort to pay the loan, making it a higher priority than maybe some other expense that comes up.

Your student loan lender is not your friend, certainly. But in many ways, the lender can do more for you than you think. In fact, for some student loans, the lender may actually forgive the whole loan. There are loads of things the student loan lender can do to help you. And what the lender asks of you is pretty simple:

1. Know your responsibilities.
2. Know your options.
3. Stay in touch.

Let's look more closely at each of these.

Know Your Responsibilities

What are the terms of the loan? Sounds like a pretty simple question, doesn't it? But it's a lot more complex and is made up of many questions: How much do you owe? When do you have to pay it back? What interest are you being charged? How much is each payment? Are they monthly payments? What happens if you don't pay? What if you can't pay? Can you extend the amount of time to pay it back? Can you pay a different amount? Who do you pay? If you go to graduate school, can you borrow more? If you have multiple loans, do you have to make multiple payments? And there are tons of other questions that you should be prepared to answer.

Borrowing is a serious commitment. Knowing your responsibilities is one of the most important steps you can take to make sure this loan doesn't come back to bite you. And if you don't know your responsibilities, chances are pretty high that the loan will cause you some grief.

So how do you learn your responsibilities? The most obvious thing is to read the promissory note. Yes, we know it's a lot of legalese, the party of the first part and the party of the second part, and so on. It really is not that confusing and there are many resources that state your responsibilities in clear language. One of the best resources is the lender itself. And in most of the cases, the lender is the federal government.

For clearly written descriptions of your rights and responsibilities as a borrower of federal loans, go to studentloans.gov (https://studentloans.gov/myDirectLoan/index.action). There you will find just about everything you need to know in non-legalese language.

Know Your Options

As I said earlier, just as you would shop around for the best mortgage and research all the terms, interest rate, and schedules involved, you should also know as much as you can about the loan options you have. Earlier in this book, I described the different loans available, including the federal loans that are awarded based on need and those for which need is not a criterion for eligibility. There are also many private lenders that offer student loans at competitive rates. When it comes to repayment terms, federal loans will likely be unmatched because of the many payment plans available, as well as the other benefits such as grace periods, deferments, forgiveness programs, and consolidation. But among private loans, there are a myriad of options for students and parents. Making the right choice may not be simple, but the rewards for choosing the best loan are ample. Again, for most students, the federal loans will be the best option. But parents need to weigh a range of factors including their credit rating and ability to qualify. Home equity loans and lines of credit have traditionally been the best option because of the tax deferment that goes along with it. But there are also many downsides to getting a home equity loan, not the least of which is putting your home at risk.

Stay in Touch

Every lender will tell you that the most important responsibility you have when you borrow is to stay in touch with the lender. After graduation, borrowers of federal loans qualify for a grace period of six months before they have to begin paying back their loans. But students and recent graduates move around a lot, so it's very possible that the correspondence between the lender and borrower (now no longer a student) will fall through one of those big cracks. That can lead to some very distressing outcomes, so I strongly encourage borrowers to be vigilant about providing contact details to their lenders. I also strongly encourage setting up an automatic payment so you never have to write a check. The money will get transferred directly out of your checking account—always the right amount, and always on time (assuming you keep enough money to prevent bounced checks). In addition, if you set up an automatic payment of a federal student loan, you usually qualify for an interest rate decrease of 0.25 percent. But even if you don't set up an auto payment, you should always notify your lender of your whereabouts.

Furthermore, if there is ever a problem preventing you from making your payment, rather than ignore the problem, you should make it a point to speak to one of the customer service representatives at the company that services your loan. Those professionals make sure you know your rights but also provide guidance on deferments, forbearance, alternative payment plans, and forgiveness programs. In this case, the customer service rep really is your friend. Their goal is to find ways for you to pay back your loan and do so over the long haul. They are trained to help you achieve that goal. The penalties for not paying your loan can be severe, and generally the federal government will win that battle. So rather than ignore the loan, it's best to be open and honest with your lender.

Appropriate Levels of Debt

No one can tell you how much is appropriate to borrow. But we can offer you guidance to help you make that decision. First off, you have to consider your own attitude about borrowing. To use the earlier example, if owing your friend a few bucks gnaws at you until you pay it back, just think how much owing thousands of dollars will keep you tossing and turning at night. Similarly, if you're one of those who is not bothered by upcoming bills, cash flow, or knowing you have obligations, you'll likely have much less reaction—and maybe even a positive one—to borrowing to pay for your or your child's college education.

Most people fall somewhere in the middle of these two extremes, and I will confess that I lean in the direction of the latter approach. That is, I think it's often a smart thing to borrow money, especially for an important investment like a college education. Although there are no guarantees, the chances are pretty good that by getting that schooling, you'll be in a better position to earn enough to pay back your loan and then some. I hope I've made this point clear: not only will you likely earn a whole lot more over your lifetime, but the quality of your life will likely be greater with an education. And more important, your kids' lives will be better. The data makes it clear that children of parents with a college education are much more likely to go on to college.

But that doesn't really answer the question of how much to borrow.

Certainly you don't want to borrow more than you need. And if you're receiving any need-based financial aid, you can pretty much be guaranteed that you won't be allowed to borrow more than you need, especially from subsidized loan programs. And admittedly, the need will be kept to a minimum, based on the cost of education.

You also don't want to borrow less than you need unless you can find alternatives to borrowing, many of which are discussed in this book. Lack of enough money to make it through college is a major cause of dropping out.

Here is a list of questions you should ask yourself before you jump into borrowing to pay for your or your child's college education.

Ten Questions to Ask Yourself Before Borrowing

1. What alternatives are there to borrowing?

   Borrowing should be the last option. Try to maximize other resources such as merit-based aid, earnings, gifts, 529 plans, employee benefits, and even part-time enrollment.

2. Can my parents help out instead of me borrowing?

   This should be a family decision and parents might be able to tap deeper into their resources more easily than students. But they should be careful to not raid their retirement savings—there's no financial aid for retirement!

3. Will my parents qualify for a home equity line of credit?

   There are many advantages of getting a home equity line of credit instead of a student loan, including lower interest rates and tax deductibility. But they also should be careful to not over borrow and risk losing their home.

4. What's the least amount I can borrow?

   Rather than borrowing as much as you can, borrow just what you need. However, don't go too low, or you'll find yourself scrambling to pay your bills and having to find part-time work that will take away from your studies.

5. Will I need to borrow for every year in college?

   You need to be thinking about your entire college career, not just the first year. Chances are, you'll need to borrow each of your four years. And maybe even a fifth year if you don't manage to graduate in four. Make sure you total up the entire amount, not just the first year.

6. Do I plan to go to graduate school for which I will need to borrow more?

   There's very little grant aid available to graduate students, so most grad students rely heavily on loans.

Keep that in mind when you start borrowing so you don't wind up borrowing more than you can handle.

7. Do I qualify for need-based financial aid?

   If you do qualify for need-based aid, there will be limits on the amount you can borrow (a good thing), and you'll also qualify for a subsidized loan (an even better thing).

8. Will I be able to qualify for a subsidized loan?

   The benefit of a subsidized loan is that interest does not accrue while you are in school or in a grace period. That could save you thousands of dollars. With unsubsidized loans, the interest begins to accrue immediately, and although you can defer payments, that interest gets added on to your principal. By the time you graduate, the amount you owe from that first year will jump significantly.

9. What will I major in (i.e., what are my prospects for a high-paying job)?

   The problem with student loans is not necessarily that students are borrowing too much, it's that too many who borrow are not finishing school, are going to schools with poor track records for employment opportunities (e.g., the for-profit schools), or are majoring in areas that don't lead to good jobs. Those who go on to grad school, for example, and have more debt, have an easier time, even if their debt is larger. In addition, if your major is one that is particularly attractive to employers, not only will you start with a higher salary, but an employer might offer to pay down your student loan as an incentive for you to join that organization.

10. Will I be going into a field where I might qualify for loan forgiveness?

    There are many professions that don't pay particularly well (teaching, for example) but offer loan forgiveness. And there are some professions—law, for example—that pay well in some places but not in others (clerking for a judge, for example) that offer loan forgiveness.

There's no simple answer as to how much is appropriate for you and your family to borrow. You have to think carefully and do some calculations. The key to knowing the appropriate amount for you is knowing what your repayment options are. After all, it's not the total amount you owe that affects your life but the amount you have to pay every month.

So to add even more confusion, you have to look at what your repayment options are. The good news is that you have many choices, including some that require you pay only a small percentage of your income. And even more good news is that there are online calculators to help you decide on the right plan.

Once we review the different plans, we can go further into discussing the appropriate level of debt for both student and parent borrowers.

🎓 Repayment Plans

The good news for borrowers is that there are many options to choose from when deciding on your repayment plan. The bad news is that there are *many* options to choose from, so you'll need to consider what's best for you.

On the www.studentloans.gov site, there is a handy-dandy calculator to help you determine the amount you'll have to pay under each of the repayment plan scenarios. If you've already received loans, then you know your totals under each program. If you're not sure, you can go to the www.nslds.ed.gov site to get an accurate and official tally.

Assuming that you have not yet started school so you don't have a portfolio for which to calculate your monthly payments, we have made some assumptions.

Let's review all the options and go more into depth about each one.

Standard Repayment

If you don't specify a different plan, you will be assigned the standard repayment plan. Under this plan, you pay the same amount each month for the total term of one hundred twenty months (ten years). The last payment might be less of course. Keep in mind that if you only borrow subsidized loans, no interest will have accrued since you first took out your first loan in your freshman year. So if you borrowed $3,500 the first year, $4,500 the second year, and $5,500 for each of the last two years, you'll owe a total of $19,000. Interest will not begin to accrue for six months after you leave school. For that amount, with an interest rate of 4.66 percent (the current rate), you'll be paying $199 per month for all one hundred twenty payments. The total amount of interest you'll have paid after ten years is $4,850. If the total amount you owe is significantly less and the calculated payment is less than $50 per month, you'll still have to pay the minimum of $50 per month. The standard repayment plan is generally the plan for which you pay the least amount of interest, so if you can handle the payments—that is, the amount of the payment doesn't affect your quality of life once you're working—it is often the best choice.

If you also have unsubsidized loans, as many students do, and your total debt is like the average graduate from a four-year school ($26,900, with $7,900 of that being an unsubsidized loan), your monthly payment jumps to $281 per month. The total amount of interest you'll have paid is $8,617.

Graduated Repayment

Under the graduated repayment plan, your payments start out below the amount of a standard plan but increase every two years. The concept is to address the fact that for most people, your salary starts out low and increases over time. Because you are actually not paying the fully amortized amount early on, you wind up paying more in interest over the long run. But for the first few years, your payments are more manageable. You still pay monthly for ten years, but the amount increases every two years.

Using the same numbers as above—that is, $19,000 in subsidized loan and $7,900 in unsubsidized loan, both at 4.66 percent, the current rate—your monthly payment for the first two years would be only $159 per month. However, by the ninth and tenth year of repayment, you'll be paying $476 per month, or three times as much. And the total amount of interest you'll have paid over the course of ten years is $8,617.

The graduated payment plan is a nice option, especially for those borrowers whose initial salary is low but who also feel confident their income will increase substantially over time.

Income-Driven Repayment plans

To assist borrowers who may not earn enough to pay the required minimum on their federal student loans, the US Department of Education offers plans that allow borrowers to pay only a specific portion of their discretionary income. New borrowers can choose from among four plans; those who have an outstanding balance on a federal student loan are restricted based on the type of loan. If you have a balance, check with your loan servicer to determine which plans you are eligible for.

Each of the income-driven plans are based on the borrower's "discretionary income," which is specifically defined for each plan and takes into account income, family size, and state of residence. The plans use the federal poverty guide-lines as a guide and they can be checked at www.aspe.hhs .gov/poverty.

REPAYE Plan

Under the Revised Pay as Your Earn Repayment (REPAYE) plan, you are required to pay no more than 10 percent of your discretionary income. This is defined as the difference between your income and 150 percent of the poverty guide-lines for your family size for people who live in your state. You can remain under this plan for twenty years if all the loans you're paying are for undergraduate school and twenty-five years if any of the loans were for graduate or professional study. After the repayment period, any remaining balance is forgiven. Note that if your loan is forgiven, that amount is considered by the IRS to be taxable income, so you may be liable for taxes. Still, for the ability to not have to pay more than you can afford, this plan can help most borrowers avoid delinquency and default.

For our borrower who owes $26,900, we estimated the annual income to be $25,000 per year and a family size of one. For that individual, the REPAYE plan monthly payment is just $60 per month. After twenty years at that same sal-ary (not likely), the borrower will have paid only $14,400, much of which is interest, so the principal will not have been reduced. In fact, because the monthly payment is not even the amount of interest accrued, the principal will have grown substantially. Potentially, at the end of the twenty-year repayment period, the borrower could owe $48,000 or more. Then again, if that amount is forgiven, the borrower will no longer owe that amount but, based on current tax law, will owe taxes on the $48,000.

Furthermore, if the borrower's income rises, the monthly payment could be $362 per month (which would be enough to pay off the loan in twenty years).

Few borrowers will stay at the $25,000 per year income range for twenty years, but it's good to know that this plan exists and may be a suitable plan for you, especially early on in your career when your salary is relatively low, or if you are entering a field that typically does not pay very well.

PAYE Plan

The Pay as Your Earn Repayment (PAYE) plan is the precursor to the above repayment plan, and much of the terms are similar to the REPAYE plan. Under the terms of the PAYE plan, borrowers still are not required to pay more than 10 percent of their discretionary income, but in addition, they are also not required to pay any more than what the standard monthly payment plan would require.

Using the borrower who owes $26,900 and earns $25,000 per year, the initial monthly payment is the same as above—that is, $60 per month. However, as we pointed out, under the REPAYE plan, if the borrower's income rises, they could be paying $362 per month. Under the PAYE plan, however, this borrower would not have to pay any more than $281 per month, the standard payment amount. At the end of twenty years, the borrower would still owe about $12,000, and that amount would be forgiven. Again, that forgiveness under current tax law is taxable income.

Income-Based Repayment (IBR)

IBR is an older plan that has many of the same features of the newer plans. Under the IBR plan, you are required to pay no more than 10 percent of your discretionary income (again, defined as the difference between your income and 150 percent of the poverty guidelines) and not more than what you would have to pay under the standard plan. For new borrowers, the term is the same twenty years. However, if you borrowed before July 1, 2014, the repayment term is twenty-five years.

Our new borrower from above would pay $60 per month and never more than $281 and might get as much as $12,000 forgiven. But a borrower with an older loan would have twenty-five years to pay off the loan, would be required to pay a minimum of $90 per month, and because of the additional five years, would not have any balance left.

Income-Contingent Repayment (ICR)

The oldest income-driven plan, ICR, has many different and less generous benefits for borrowers. First, the definition of discretionary income is different. Under ICR, discretionary income is defined as the difference between your income and 100 percent of the poverty guidelines. Second, the monthly payments are either the amount you would pay on a twelve-year (not ten-year) standard plan multiplied for an income percentage factor, or 20 percent (not 10 percent) of discretionary income, whichever is less. In the case of our borrower owing $26,900 with an annual salary of $25,000, the monthly payment would be $163. As a result, there would be no balance after twenty years, so there would be no forgiveness.

Needless to say, deciding from among four income-driven plans, plus the standard and graduated payment plans, is not an easy task. And each of these is complicated. The good news is that there really is help available to guide you in your decision. And, of course, it's always possible to change payment plans later on. However, that too is not a simple task, so it's generally best to figure out early on which plan is the most reasonable for you.

To help you decide, you can use the US Department of Education's repayment estimator at https://studentloans.gov/myDirectLoan/mobile/repayment/repaymentEstimator.action#view-repayment-plans&ui-state=dialog. You can also check with the servicer of your student loans. The customer service representatives are there to help you make a wise decision based on your individual circumstances.

Table 6.1: Sample Repayment Plans

Repayment plan	First monthly payment	Last monthly payment	Total amount paid	Projected loan forgiveness	Repayment period
Standard	$281	$281	$33,767	$0	120 months
Graduated	$159	$476	$35,517	$0	120 months
Revised Pay As You Earn (REPAYE)	$60	$362	$48,249	$0	271 months
Pay As You Earn (PAYE)	$60	$281	$37,928	$11,916	240 months
Income-based repayment (IBR)	$90	$281	$43,338	$0	216 months
IBR for new borrowers	$60	$281	$37,928	$11,916	240 months
Income-contingent repayment (ICR)	$163	$208	$41,062	$0	222 months

Appropriate Levels of Student Debt

As several economists and researchers have written, the trouble with student loans is not necessarily the high level of debt, but the low earnings of borrowers. And further, the problem is not necessarily about those who borrow the highest amounts. Default rates are actually highest among those who have the smallest debts—that is, less than $5,000. And the rate decreases as the debt level goes up. Seems backward, doesn't it? But if you think this through, it makes total sense. Those who borrow the most (with some odd exceptions) are those who go onto graduate or professional school. And, of course, they earn a lot more than those with just a bachelor's degree. In turn, graduates with a bachelor's degree generally earn more than those with an associate's degree, a trade school certificate, or no degree at all. Furthermore, the borrowers who default the most are those who went to either one of the for-profit schools or community colleges and so weren't in school long enough to rack up high levels of debt. They are also the ones who have the most difficulty finding jobs.

So while I am in no way minimizing the impact student loans may have on recent graduates, it's clear that there are many ways to face that issue. One way is for borrowers to use one of the income-driven repayment plans that are described above.

Forbearance

A second way to manage your loans is built into the programs themselves. Every borrower has the opportunity to ask for forbearance. If you are willing but unable to pay, you can ask the loan servicer to grant you a forbearance, which means you can stop making payments, or reduce the amount you pay, for up to twelve months. Interest will continue to accrue, but you will not be delinquent nor be placed in default. Forbearances are granted by the lender, and you will need to demonstrate a financial hardship or an illness that is preventing you from having sufficient funds.

Deferments

There are also periods when you can defer payments on your loan. These are clearly spelled out in the loan documents and reviewed in the entrance and exit interviews borrowers are required to go through. If you are enrolled in school at least half-time, whether that's undergraduate or graduate, or on active duty military during a war or national emergency, you can get a deferment. During that period, you are not required to make any payments on your loans. Interest on unsubsidized loans does continue to accrue during periods of deferment, but interest on subsidized loans *does not* accrue. To qualify for a deferment, you must apply to your loan servicer and be certain that you continue to make payments until the deferment (or forbearance) is granted.

None of these options deal with the basic question of how much to borrow. But they all affect the decision.

How Much Can I Afford to Borrow?

The question really boils down to how much you can afford to pay back after all the options have been considered. As we made clear, there is no hard and fast rule, especially when you consider that different types of loans have different terms and interest rates. Furthermore, some borrowers are more comfortable with higher debt, some less so. Some borrowers will also have a car loan and credit card debt, while others will not be making payments on any other outstanding balance. But for a quick guestimate, here's a helpful table that shows amounts of loan and the percentage of take-home pay it would require with different salaries.

Table 6.2: Loan Amount and Salary Required to Pay

Loan amount	Monthly payment	Salary required	Percent take-home pay
$25,000	$150	$25,000	10%
$50,000	$450	$45,000	16%
$75,000	$750	$60,000	20%

Remember, though, that student borrowers have the option of selecting one of the income-driven repayment plans that may make the monthly payment more affordable. Although there is no standard for an appropriate amount of loan, it is often suggested that a person's rent or mortgage, combined with payments for student loans, car loans, credit card balances, and all other debts, should not be more than 40 percent of take-home pay. If your student loan balance puts you over the top, you should strongly consider one of the income-driven repayment plans.

🎓 Appropriate Levels of Parent Debt

Helping to pay for your child's education by borrowing is certainly a time-honored tradition, but with costs skyrocketing and other pressures brought upon families, there is great concern about the level of debt parents are undertaking. The good news is that there are many programs available to parents, including some that do not require high credit scores. The bad news is that many parents are burying themselves in debt at levels worse than their children.

As we discussed earlier, parents of undergraduate students can borrow through the Direct PLUS Loan program. Other options are home equity lines of credit (HELOC), retirement account loans, investment account loans, and personal lines of credit. Lenders seem to be thrilled to loan to parents, especially those who can and do pay it all back. After all, that's how banks make their money.

The key is to know how much to borrow and, if it seems you're going to go over that amount, how to find alternatives.

What's the right amount? Well, to repeat what was written above about total debt, people should not be paying more than about 40 percent of their monthly take-home pay for outstanding debt. In years past, the standard was 33 percent maximum on mortgage and 7 percent on all other debts, including car loans, credit cards, student loans, and so on. That standard has changed, and there is less division between mortgage and other debts. While the total suggested debt can be higher, it is ill-advised for people to pay more than 50 percent of their monthly income on their debts.

Furthermore, most financial advisors feel strongly that parents should not borrow from their retirement accounts to pay for their children's education because they are leaving themselves in poor shape for their later years. As many people have found out (often the hard way) being house rich—that is, owing little or nothing on their home but not having much in the way of liquid assets—can be a problem when your income is reduced. While paying down the balance on your mortgage is a worthy goal, people need to keep an open mind about maintaining a mortgage balance, or at least have access to a home equity line of credit. Cash flow while children are in college can pose major problems for parents. A PLUS Loan is certainly one way to counter that. But with a 6 percent or more interest rate and, even more important, a 4 percent or more fee, many people should look for less expensive alternatives if their credit scores and other debts qualify them.

Consolidation and Refinancing

In the mortgage industry, homeowners are often encouraged to refinance their mortgage when interest rates go down. Even when you add in the cost of the refi, as it's called, that low cost will be made up within the first year or two. If your mortgage is $2,000 per month, for example, with an interest rate of 5 percent, refinancing at 4 percent could lower your mortgage to $1,600 per month, a $400 per month savings. Even if it cost you $5,000 to refinance, in just over a year you'll have made that money back, and for the rest of the loan you'll have saved $400 each month.

The same could theoretically be true with student loans, although refinancing student loans is generally not a very good idea because the interest rates are not likely to be lower. Furthermore, by refinancing, you will be losing all the other benefits of a federal student loan, including deferments and forgiveness provisions, but especially the income-driven repayment plans that allow you to pay smaller amounts.

If you have taken out private loans to pay for your child's education, however, it might be beneficial to look at ways of refinancing those loans at a lower rate. That might not be possible unless you decide to take out a home equity loan, which will likely have a lower rate than a private, unsecured student loan. In addition, as I pointed out earlier, when you borrow against the value of your home, there is always the risk of losing your home, albeit a small risk.

But there are, certainly, a number of lenders that will refinance your student loans. When considering those, you need to know the answers to a few important questions:

1. What interest rate will I get? Note that the rate you get will be tied to your credit history and credit scores.
2. What is my goal in refinancing? If you have multiple loans, each of which requires a monthly payment, you may be simply looking to consolidate your loans, not refinance them. There are federal consolidation options that you should consider.
3. What benefits am I giving up? If it's possible you'll be going to graduate school, you will be giving up the possibility of in-school deferments. And with a private loan, you won't be eligible for the income-driven loan repayment plans offered to federal student loan borrowers.

Consolidation

As I discussed in chapter three, the federal government offers a Direct Consolidation Loan that allows you to lump all the federal loans you owe into one new one. Note that only federal student loans and Direct PLUS Loans can be consolidated into the Direct Consolidation Loan. The benefit of consolidation is that you will then have just one monthly payment instead of multiple payments. And sometimes, because of minimum monthly payments on the loans, that one payment could be less than the sum of all the others. That can certainly help your budget. In addition, the federal Direct Consolidation Loan is eligible for certain of the income-driven repayment plans, which means you will not be overburdened by the monthly payments. Furthermore, the repayment term for Direct Consolidation Loans can be as much as thirty years, which could further reduce the monthly payment amount. The interest rate you pay is the weighted average of the underlying loans rounded up to the nearest 1 percent, and the interest rate is fixed for the life of the loan.

Although there are some benefits of consolidating, you may be giving up certain benefits that you have with the underlying loans. For example, if you return to school or go to graduate school, you will not be able to get a deferment, whereas subsidized student loans qualify for in-school deferments. Second, consolidation loans are not eligible for certain loan forgiveness or cancellation benefits that the underlying loans may be eligible for.

That said, if you wind up paying multiple payments each month for different loans, you might seriously consider consolidating. You can choose from among several repayment plan options, including one of the income-driven plans. There is no fee to consolidate and you can easily calculate the amount you'd have to pay monthly by going to https://studentaid.ed.gov/sa/repay-loans/consolidation. Just remember that only federal student or parent loans can be consolidated into a Direct Consolidation Loan.

CHAPTER 7

Graduate School, Alternative Paths, and Other Considerations

Natala Hart, former director of financial aid at The Ohio State University, applied her Diaper Savings Theory. When her daughter stopped wearing disposable diapers, the family experienced a significant pay increase, so they put that savings into their daughter's college fund.

As we discussed earlier, you can't just look at paying for college as a one-time expenditure. First, very few families can afford to pay the large expense out of their current income. And for most people, even if they have the money, it's not a very good idea to take it all out of savings, especially if that savings is targeted for retirement. To make things more complicated, there are some other considerations you should focus on when thinking about how to finance your or your child's education. Here are a few of those factors.

Graduate School

One factor you'll need to consider when determining how much to borrow for college is your plan once you finish your undergraduate degree. Entering your first year is not always the easiest time to figure out your plan for the rest of your life. But it is a question that you need to consider at least a little.

If you think you'll be going on for more education, then you need to know that most of the aid available to graduate students is in the form of loans. Although you are automatically considered "independent" for financial aid purposes (except for many medical schools and some law schools), and have demonstrated need, there is just very little grant aid for graduate students. In addition, chances are, your parents are not going to help support you in graduate school, and even if you find a fellowship, assistantship, or some other source of income, the rest of the costs are mostly going to be borne by loans.

Of course, with a graduate or professional degree, your starting salary when you finish is likely to be significantly higher than with just a bachelor's degree. That will allow you afford higher monthly payments. And the good news in that regard is that there are federal student loans available to you as a graduate student.

But going back to the real question of how much to borrow to help pay for your bachelor's degree, give serious consideration to whether you might go to graduate school. That, of course, will depend on your major.

Certainly one option for continued schooling is putting off grad school until a later date. But ultimately, if you think grad school is an option, be even more wary about taking large amounts of loan as an undergrad. The horror stories you hear and read about people coming out of school with more than $100,000 in debt are almost exclusively because of grad or professional school (i.e., law and medicine). Yes, there are some other examples of students with exorbitant debt levels, but as I pointed out early on, those are rare and often because the student went to multiple schools over a long period of time.

The bottom line: if you are thinking of going into a field for which you will need an advanced degree, especially if it's a field for which you need that advanced degree before entering the workplace, then keep your undergraduate loan debt lower.

For-Profit Schools and Gainful Employment

There has been a great deal of media attention paid to students who attended for-profit schools and wound up deeply in debt with little or no promise for a job that will enable them to pay back the loan. The students who attend some of these schools are enticed by promises of great jobs after they finish, only to find out that the job market is not quite as strong as they were led to believe. In fact, the US Department of Education has taken steps to ensure that students are getting what they paid for. Now, under federal regulations, career schools must offer certificate or degree programs that prepare students for "gainful employment in a recognized occupation." If the typical graduate's loan payments exceed 20 percent of his or her discretionary income or 8 percent of total income, the school could lose eligibility for federal student aid.

Although there are many excellent career schools— ones that really do teach the kinds of skills needed to succeed in specific fields—there are also a great many schools that are not quite so legitimate. The students who graduate with degrees or certificates from the good schools go on to good jobs and careers. Sadly, though, too many students who attend career schools either do not finish the program or do not qualify for the good jobs. And unfortunately, most students who attend these schools have to take out loans because the costs are high (they are equivalent to many of the more traditional private colleges) but they don't offer as much grant aid. One measure of the quality of these schools is the default rate: the group of borrowers with the highest default rate is the group that attended the career colleges. That should alert you to a problem. I can't stress enough that you should think carefully before you decide to borrow to attend a for-profit career college, even if that college offers a traditional bachelor's degree program. Think about whether you can obtain that same education and degree at a less expensive school where you don't need to borrow so much.

An excellent tool you have to evaluate the for-profit school is the data it has about job placement. But don't just accept the rate the school publishes. Look more carefully at the rate of recent graduates if the school offers that data. And also make sure the school is reporting only graduates who work *in the field of study*. Too often the job placement rate includes people who are working in fast food jobs or something similar, not in the field they paid to learn about. Yes, those people have jobs. But I don't think that's the kind of job you'll want to consider after you pay thousands of dollars for your education. And, of course, if there has been action taken by the US Department of Education against the school because of gainful employment regulations not being met, you should probably find another school to attend.

🎓 Online Courses/Distance Learning

Certainly one of the newest and fastest-growing learning methods is online learning. Courses are offered by a host of colleges and universities, most of which are in the for-profit sector, although many of those colleges also partner with more traditional, not-for-profit colleges. Clearly what you are paying for with these courses is just the actual academic portion of higher education. To compare prices of these courses versus regular college costs, you must look only at tuition and fees. The prices of online courses can be as low as some of the community and state colleges or as high as the private, not-for-profit colleges and universities. Some of the courses offered are eligible for federal financial aid, while some are not. Some courses can count toward a degree, some cannot. Some courses are offered by the online division of the traditional college, and others are not. Online and distance learning is a quickly changing concept and some, like many of the for-profit career colleges, are not worth the money, while others provide high-quality instruction at reasonable prices.

One way that these online courses can be a big benefit is in accelerating the time it takes to complete a degree. That, in turn, may lower your overall costs. So, for example, if you take a traditional course load of 30 credits per year, it would take four years to complete the 120-credit degree. But if you can squeeze in one or two online courses per year, perhaps taken during school breaks or summers, that could save you one entire semester's worth at your college. Will that save you money? Perhaps. It would definitely mean graduating early so you could enter the workforce sooner.

However, you'd be paying for the online courses instead of the traditional courses, so the amount may not be substantially different. And since there's usually very little financial aid available for online courses other than loans, that would add to your total debt. Furthermore, at many colleges, you pay a flat fee regardless of the number of credits you take. So accelerating by taking online courses for which you pay extra may wind up costing you more!

Most important, if you are considering online courses, be certain the credits can count toward your degree. And be certain that the online courses are accredited.

🎓 Independent and Nontraditional Students

More than half of the students attending college in the United States are nontraditional students—that is, they are older and independent of their parents. Many of these students go part-time to school and work part-or full-time.

As we said at the very beginning of the discussion about the financial aid application process, one of the first things you do is determine whether the applicant is dependent or independent. That determines who has the primary responsibility for paying the costs of education.

In order to claim you are independent, you must meet one of the following conditions:

- be more than twenty-four years old
- be a veteran of the US Armed Forces
- be enrolled in a graduate or professional program
- be married
- be an orphan or a ward of the court
- have legal dependents (other than a spouse)

If you meet any of these criteria, you are considered independent, and your parent's income does not count toward your expected family contribution.

There can be other exceptions made on a case-by-case basis by the financial aid office at the college. Unwillingness to pay is not considered a reason to make an exception. Even if parents and children are estranged, unless it can be documented that there's an adverse situation, the college is not likely to make an exception with regard to dependency. The reasoning is clear: you'd be asking the taxpayers to pay instead of your parents. As a taxpayer, you'd want the same good stewardship of your funds.

But if you do meet the criteria or an exception is made, the entire application process changes. Instead of reporting parents' income, you're evaluated by only your (and your spouse's) income. To complicate the issue, the base year is not the current or prior year, but two years before (e.g., 2015 income for a 2017 enrollment). Clearly a lot can change in that time, especially for older, independent students. One of the key things to remember is that when you are completing the Free Application for Federal Student Aid (FAFSA) and CSS PROFILE, you report the situation as of the date you complete the application. For example, while you may have been single two years ago, if you got married yesterday, you report that you're married. This is when things get complicated and require more individual instruction. This assistance is available online when you're completing the FAFSA, so check all the help screens if you fit into one of the more complicated situations.

You might also explain your situation to the financial aid office staff as you get further into the application process. Financial aid administrators routinely make exceptions about whose income to use when marital or parent status changes.

One other thing to consider if you are declared independent is that your income is very likely going to change as soon as you enroll in college. Even if you made a decent living in the past, once you enroll, you'll likely lose a significant portion, if not all, of your income. That means you'll then have to estimate how much you anticipate earning during the current term, which generally crosses calendar years. If you're enrolling in fall of 2017 for the 2017–18 academic year, you may have had a full-time job for most of 2017. But to enroll, you leave your job and your income becomes zero (and yes, it's perfectly acceptable to say zero). And your winter/spring 2018 income is also expected to be zero. So when estimating your current year, be realistic. If you have no job, then say zero. Don't presume you'll get a job unless you actually have one. (Ideally, you'll be able to find a way to work part-time at your current job, since you'll likely earn more there than at some work-study or new job.)

Again, be realistic, not overly optimistic. Don't say "Well, I know I'm going to have to have a certain amount of money, so I'll estimate that I'll earn this much." You only report what you have and what you expect to have.

Lastly, returning to school can be a major adjustment for many people. For those who haven't been a student for some time, the difference in lifestyle and daily existence is stressful and difficult. Don't underestimate how tough it will be to balance school and work, kids, your precious time, outside pressures, and deadlines. Focus on the goal, seek guidance and counseling to help you through the tough times, and beg forgiveness from those around you as you plod along as a student. Remember that your loved ones, especially your children, will gain so much from your commitment to furthering your education. You'll be that great role model your children most need and respect.

Alternate Paths

Gap Years

College is not for everybody. And certainly it's not for everybody at a particular time in one's life. I think I'm a great example of a person who probably should have taken a little time doing something other than continuing my schooling right after high school. I was younger than most of my classmates because I had skipped a grade. And I was even immature for my age. I didn't know it then, but as I reflect back, I would have been better off had I experienced something other than school before jumping in. This was before ADHD became a household word. My parents certainly would not have supported this: they were bound and determined that I attend college. And growing up, that was always the expectation.

My brother had gone and so would I. I was fortunate that my parents had scrimped and saved so they could send me to college without me having to borrow. I did work during college, but only for one of the years. And I took out a loan for graduate school. I managed to finish my undergraduate degree in four years, but it was not easy. In fact, it was quite a struggle. I barely made it though, and only did so because of some great support from some wonderful faculty guidance. I didn't graduate with honors. In fact, I graduated very close to the bottom of my class. That surprised a lot of people because I was one of the top students in high school. I went to a top school, I had the ability to succeed, but I didn't have the maturity or discipline that excelling required.

I'm sharing my personal story so those of you who relate to my college experience don't feel alone. I was a lousy college student. I was smart and could pull together assignments at the last minute that got me through. I had the same approach in high school, but it wasn't as challenging so I was able to get away with it. By the time I got to college, though, I realized that everyone there was smart. Much smarter than me, in fact. And they knew how to study. I only knew how to pull together something acceptable at the last minute. But that's not okay when you're at a top school.

Going to college is a commitment you have to make individually, not one that can be assigned to you. Some of you reading this may not have had the expectation all your life that you would go to college. For you, I say *Go to college*. You will gain so much and your life will change so much by doing so. Yes it will be tough. Yes you'll have times when you will regret the decision. But your life will be better for it. I guarantee that.

For those who did have the expectation that you'd go on to college but you're not sure, you're in a different category. Ask yourself why you're not sure. Is it because you don't know what you want to do with the rest of your life? Well, duh, who does? Especially as a young person. Sure, there are some people who are committed and know they'll go to medical school or be a lawyer, engineer, singer, dancer, artist, whatever. If you're not in this group, rest assured that neither are most of your peers. There's one thing that's especially great about college: you get to try something on. If it fits, it's yours, even if it was someone else's in your family before you. *If it fits, it's yours.*

But if there's some other reason you're not sure you want to go straight from high school to college, what is it you *do* want to do? There are certainly a lot of options, so maybe now's a great time to think about those options.

Is money the reason you're considering not going? I hope I assured you in this book that there will be enough money if you need it, even if you have to take out loans. You *will* be able to pay them back. And your life will not be ruined by having those debts.

Does something else attract you more? Wow, aren't you lucky. If it's something you can commit to, that's great. If it's serving in some foreign land helping the world, that's quite a challenge and quite admirable. Think it through carefully, talk to the people around you who care about you, and make a rational decision. You can go to college later and be all the better for having taken that time to do something mean-ingful. You'll have grown by the experience, and when you do decide to further your education, you'll likely excel and bring great knowledge to the classroom.

If you're unsure about whether you can handle the college work, I urge you to try it. You will not be alone. Most everyone there, whether it's at a top-rated school or your local commu-nity college, will have many of those same doubts. Take the plunge, try your best, and seek help and guidance when you need it. Teachers are there to teach, and most relish the idea of opening up a student's mind to learning. Every college has guidance counselors who can help when you run into barriers. The most highly rated and competitive colleges have staff devoted to making sure you succeed. These colleges accept the best and brightest. They know each student can make it academically. If a bright student is having difficulty, it must be because of some other pressure or issue; it's not about his or her ability to do the work.

The same is true at just about every college. The commitment you make to going to college and succeeding there is matched by the faculty and staff at the colleges themselves. They want to see you graduate just as much as you want to graduate.

Military Service

One of the wonderful alternate paths young people can take is serving in the military. Yes, it's tough, but the rewards are great, not the least of which is the ability to qualify for veterans educational benefits you can use to attend college. But there is also the learning you'll do while in service. There are unparalleled opportunities to learn technical skills. There are unique opportunities to learn about international affairs and diplomacy. These go hand-in-hand with other critical learning skills like discipline and time management. You can serve in the military for as long as you want. And as an added bonus, you also are paid for your service. If a gap year is a consideration for you, serving in the military is one option you might think about.

Peace Corps

If serving humanity is something that attracts you, serving in the Peace Corps is a great option. As with military service, the rewards are great and the learning opportunities unmatched. Founded in 1961, the Peace Corps mission "to promote world peace and friendship" is as relevant now as it was more than fifty years ago. More than 200,000 volunteers live and work in communities around the world, serving residents in numerous ways. Almost every volunteer has something positive to say about the experience and many return to serve again. The commitment is for two years, and in some instances, the service can count toward a master's degree.

If this kind of opportunity and work appeals to you, you can get more information by visiting www.peacecorps.org.

Internships

In lieu of or in conjunction with attending college part-time, you may want to consider being an intern. What exactly is that? Simply put, it is an opportunity to work for an employer and learn the trade, so to speak. These "jobs" may be paid or volunteer, but in either case can provide valuable experience that can later lead to a full-time job. Some may even offer college credit. Generally internships are short-term or, at least, are for a defined period of time. And neither the intern nor the employer is bound to continue after the term is expired. Parenthetically, apprenticeships are similar in that there is a transfer of knowledge and skills from the professional to the apprentice, but in that case, there is an implied understanding that once apprentices learn enough, they will work for the professional.

There are numerous internships available in just about every discipline, some with private companies, some with government agencies, and some with nonprofit organizations. You can learn more about these and apply for an internship by Googling "internships" or by visiting http://www.internships.com/student.

Travel

Few people can avail themselves of this kind of gap year opportunity, but for those who have the resources, world travel can be learning at its best. Experiencing different cultures and seeing the world through the eyes of other people will awaken parts of you like no other experience. Ideally you'll not only visit tourist areas but also meet and live with people in other countries for extended periods. From that, you'll gain a perspective that you'll be able to bring to the educational world when you do decide to go to college. You'll be able to participate in class discussions and provide insight that other students will not have.

At the same time, there is some danger with taking a gap year to travel. You lose your "student edge," the ability to study and do assignments that maybe are not as exciting as what you experienced when traveling. That's a small price to pay, I think, for gaining the kind of firsthand knowledge of the world. And chances are that when you do go on to college, either in the United States or abroad, you'll do so with a much better commitment to completing the work.

If you're one of the few who can take time off to travel instead of going straight to college from high school, I encourage you to consider it. But I also warn you: it might be more advantageous to take that gap year *after* you finish your undergraduate years.

Working

Getting out to the "real world," as many call it, has an appeal. The notion of being an adult, earning a living, paying your bills, and experiencing what it's like to not be a student are very attractive. Maybe for the first time in your life you'll have a few bucks in your pocket (although it's very likely you'll be living hand to mouth, since your living expenses are likely to be pretty close to what you'll be earning). Maybe the idea of not having homework assignments but rather being able to do what you want in the evenings is especially attractive to you. And maybe just getting a job—any job—is better than trying to figure out your life's work. Maybe this is your chance to "get it out of your system." You can be a ski bum or beach bum. You likely won't have another chance to do that.

But the dangers are very real, and if this is something you're considering, I urge you to think twice. As I have said repeatedly, getting that college degree will open up doors you could never open without the degree—or, more important, without the education. Your life and your children's lives will change forever. Yes, going to or back to college will mean sacrifice, especially if you've been out there earning money. You'll have created a different lifestyle, and being a student will mean living meagerly and being focused on schoolwork. Success in college takes a strong will and perseverance. But even if you're not sure, maybe dip your foot into college, push yourself through, and then consider what options you have in your life.

Appendix:

FAFSA ON THE WEB WORKSHEET

FAFSA on the Web Worksheet

2016 – 2017

www.fafsa.gov

Federal Student Aid | PROUD SPONSOR of the AMERICAN MIND®

DO NOT MAIL THIS WORKSHEET.

The *FAFSA on the Web Worksheet* provides a preview of the questions that you may be asked while completing the *Free Application for Federal Student Aid* (FAFSA®) online at **www.fafsa.gov**.

You must complete and submit a FAFSA to apply for federal student aid and for most state and college aid. Write down notes to help you easily complete your FAFSA anytime after January 1, 2016.

See the table to the right for state deadlines. Your application must be submitted by midnight Central time. Also pay attention to the symbols that may be listed after your state deadline. Check with your high school counselor or your college's financial aid administrator about other deadlines. The Federal deadline is June 30, 2017.

- **This Worksheet is optional and should only be completed if you plan to use *FAFSA on the Web.***

- **Sections in purple are for parent information.**

- **This Worksheet does not include all the questions from the FAFSA. The questions that are included are ordered as they appear on *FAFSA on the Web*. When you are online, you may be able to skip some questions based on your answers to earlier questions.**

Applying is easier with the IRS Data Retrieval Tool!

Beginning in early February 2016, students and parents who have completed their 2015 IRS tax return may be able to use *FAFSA on the Web* to electronically view their tax information. With just a few simple steps, the tax information can also be securely transferred into *FAFSA on the Web*.

Sign your FAFSA with an FSA ID!

For information about the FSA ID, including how to apply, go to **studentaid.gov/fsaid**.

Your FSA ID allows you to electronically sign your FAFSA. If you are providing parent information, one parent must also sign your FAFSA. To sign electronically, your parent should also apply for an FSA ID.

Free help is available!

You do not have to pay to get help or submit your FAFSA. Submit your FAFSA **free** online at **www.fafsa.gov**. Federal Student Aid provides **free** help online at **www.fafsa.gov** or you can call 1-800-4-FED-AID (1-800-433-3243). TTY users (hearing impaired) can call 1-800-730-8913.

NOTES:

Check with your financial aid administrator for these states and territories:
AL, AS *, AZ, CO, FM *, GA, GU *, HI *, MH *, MP *, NE, NH *, NM, PR, PW *, SD *, UT, VA *, VI *, WI and WV *.

Pay attention to any symbols listed after your state deadline.

State	Deadline
AK	Alaska Performance Scholarship - June 30, 2016; later applications accepted if funds available. Alaska Education Grant - As soon as possible after January 1, 2016. $
AR	Academic Challenge - June 1, 2016 *(date received)* Workforce Grant - Contact the financial aid office. Higher Education Opportunity Grant - June 1, 2016 *(date received)*
CA	For many state financial aid programs - March 2, 2016 *(date postmarked)* + * For additional community college Cal Grants - September 2, 2016 *(date postmarked)* + * Contact the California Student Aid Commission or your financial aid administrator for more information.
CT	February 15, 2016 *(date received)* # *
DC	FAFSA completed by May 1, 2016 *(date received)* For DCTAG, complete the DC OneApp and submit supporting documents by June 30, 2016.
DE	April 15, 2016 *(date received)*
FL	May 15, 2016 *(date processed)*
IA	July 1, 2016 *(date received)* Earlier priority deadlines may exist for certain programs. *
ID	Opportunity Grant - March 1, 2016 *(date received)* # *
IL	As soon as possible after January 1, 2016. $
IN	March 10, 2016 *(date received)*
KS	April 1, 2016 *(date received)* # *
KY	As soon as possible after January 1, 2016. $
LA	July 1, 2017 *(date received)*; July 1, 2016 recommended
MA	May 1, 2016 *(date received)* #
MD	March 1, 2016 *(date received)*
ME	May 1, 2016 *(date received)*
MI	March 1, 2016 *(date received)*
MN	30 days after term starts *(date received)*
MO	April 1, 2016 *(date received)*
MS	MTAG and MESG Grants - September 15, 2016 *(date received)* HELP Scholarship - March 31, 2016 *(date received)*
MT	March 1, 2016 *(date received)* #
NC	As soon as possible after January 1, 2016. $
ND	April 15, 2016 *(date received)* # Earlier priority deadlines may exist for institutional programs.
NJ	2015-2016 Tuition Aid Grant recipients - June 1, 2016 *(date received)* All other applicants - October 1, 2016, fall & spring terms *(date received)* - March 1, 2017, spring term only *(date received)*
NV	Silver State Opportunity Grant - As soon as possible after January 1, 2016. $ All other aid - Contact your financial aid administrator. *
NY	June 30, 2017 *(date received)* *
OH	October 1, 2016 *(date received)*
OK	March 1, 2016 *(date received)* *
OR	OSAC Private Scholarships - March 1, 2016 Oregon Opportunity Grant - As soon as possible after January 1, 2016. $
PA	All first-time applicants enrolled in a: community college; business/trade/technical school; hospital school of nursing; designated Pennsylvania Open-Admission institution; or non-transferable two-year program - August 1, 2016 *(date received)* All other applicants - May 1, 2016 *(date received)* *
RI	March 1, 2016 *(date received)* #
SC	Tuition Grants - June 30, 2016 *(date received)* SC Commission on Higher Education Need-based Grants - As soon as possible after January 1, 2016. $
TN	State Grant - March 1, 2016. Eligible prior-year recipients receive priority, and all other awards made to neediest applicants until funds are depleted. State Lottery - fall term, September 1, 2016 *(date received)*; spring & summer terms, February 1, 2017 *(date received)* Tennessee Promise - February 15, 2016
TX	March 15, 2016 *(date received)*
VT	As soon as possible after January 1, 2016. $ *
WA	As soon as possible after January 1, 2016. $
WV	PROMISE Scholarship - March 1, 2016. New applicants must submit additional application. Contact your financial aid administrator or your state agency. WV Higher Education Grant Program - April 15, 2016

For priority consideration, submit application by date specified.
+ Applicants encouraged to obtain proof of mailing.
$ Awards made until funds are depleted.
* Additional form may be required.

STATE AID DEADLINES

The Federal Student Aid logo and FAFSA are registered trademarks of Federal Student Aid, U.S. Department of Education.

Source: © 2016 The College Board. www.collegeboard.org.
Reproduced with permission.

SECTION 1 - STUDENT INFORMATION

After you are online, you can add up to ten colleges on your FAFSA. The colleges will receive the information from your processed FAFSA.

Student's Last Name	First Name	Social Security Number

Student Citizenship Status (check one of the following)

❑ U.S. citizen (U.S. national)   ❑ Neither citizen nor eligible noncitizen

❑ Eligible noncitizen (Enter your Alien Registration Number in the box to the right.)

Generally, you are an eligible noncitizen if you are:

Your Alien Registration Number

A								

- A permanent U.S. resident with a Permanent Resident Card (I-551);
- A conditional permanent resident with a Conditional Green Card (I-551C);
- The holder of an Arrival-Departure Record (I-94) from the Department of Homeland Security showing any of the following designations: "Refugee," "Asylum Granted," "Parolee" (I-94 confirms paroled for a minimum of one year and status has not expired), T-Visa holder (T-1, T-2, T-3, etc.) or "Cuban-Haitian Entrant;" or
- The holder of a valid certification or eligibility letter from the Department of Health and Human Services showing a designation of "Victim of human trafficking."

Student Marital Status (check one of the following)

❑ Single   ❑ Married or remarried   ❑ Separated   ❑ Divorced or widowed

You will be asked to provide information about your spouse if you are married or remarried.

Selective Service Registration

If you are male and 25 or younger, you can use the FAFSA to register with the Selective Service System.

What is the highest school parent 1 completed?	❑ Middle school/Jr. high	❑ College or beyond
	❑ High school	❑ Other/unknown
What is the highest school parent 2 completed?	❑ Middle school/Jr. high	❑ College or beyond
	❑ High school	❑ Other/unknown

SECTION 2 - STUDENT DEPENDENCY STATUS

If you can check ANY of the following boxes, you will not have to provide parental information. Skip to page 4.
If you check NONE of the following boxes, you will be asked to provide parental information. Go to the next page.

❑ I was born before January 1, 1993	❑ I am married	❑ I will be working on a master's or doctorate program (e.g., MA, MBA, MD, JD, PhD, EdD, graduate certificate)	
❑ I am serving on active duty in the U.S. Armed Forces	❑ I am a veteran of the U.S. Armed Forces	❑ I now have or will have children for whom I will provide more than half of their support between July 1, 2016 and June 30, 2017	
❑ Since I turned age 13, both of my parents were deceased	❑ I was in foster care since turning age 13	❑ I have dependents (other than children or my spouse) who live with me and I provide more than half of their support	
❑ I was a dependent or ward of the court since turning age 13	❑ I am currently or I was an emancipated minor	❑ I am currently or I was in legal guardianship	❑ I am homeless or I am at risk of being homeless

NOTES:

SECTION 3 - PARENT INFORMATION

Who is considered a parent? "Parent" refers to a biological or adoptive parent or a person determined by the state to be a parent (for example, if the parent is listed on the birth certificate). Grandparents, foster parents, legal guardians, older siblings, and uncles or aunts are **not** considered parents on this form unless they have legally adopted you. If your legal parents are living and married to each other, answer the questions about both of them. If your legal parents are not married and **live together**, answer the questions about both of them. In case of divorce or separation, give information about the parent you lived with most in the last 12 months. If you did not live with one parent more than the other, give information about the parent who provided you the most financial support during the last 12 months or during the most recent year you received support. If your divorced or widowed parent has remarried, also provide information about your stepparent.

Providing parent 1 information? You will need:	Providing parent 2 information? You will need:
Parent 1 (father/mother/stepparent) Social Security Number	Parent 2 (father/mother/stepparent) Social Security Number
Parent 1 (father/mother/stepparent) name	Parent 2 (father/mother/stepparent) name
Parent 1 (father/mother/stepparent) date of birth	Parent 2 (father/mother/stepparent) date of birth
❏ Check here if parent 1 is a dislocated worker	❏ Check here if parent 2 is a dislocated worker

Did you know?

If your parents file a tax return with the IRS, they may be eligible to use the IRS Data Retrieval Tool, which is the easiest way to provide accurate tax information. With just a few simple steps, they may be able to view their tax return information and securely transfer it into *FAFSA on the Web*.

Did your parents file or will they file a 2015 income tax return?

❏ My parents have already completed a tax return

❏ My parents will file, but have not yet completed a tax return

❏ My parents are not going to file an income tax return

What was your parents' adjusted gross income for 2015?

Skip this question if your parents did not file taxes. Adjusted gross income is on IRS Form 1040—Line 37; 1040A—line 21; or 1040EZ—line 4.

$ _____

The following questions ask about earnings (wages, salaries, tips, etc.) in 2015. Answer the questions whether or not a tax return was filed. This information may be on the W-2 forms, or on the IRS Form 1040—Line 7 + 12 + 18 + Box 14 (Code A) of IRS Schedule K-1 (Form 1065); 1040A—line 7; or 1040EZ—line 1.

How much did parent 1 (father/mother/stepparent) earn from working in 2015? $ _____

How much did parent 2 (father/mother/stepparent) earn from working in 2015? $ _____

In 2014 or 2015, did anyone in your parents' household receive: (Check all that apply.)

❏ Supplemental Security Income (SSI)   ❏ Temporary Assistance for Needy Families (TANF)

❏ Supplemental Nutrition Assistance Program (SNAP)   ❏ Special Supplemental Nutrition Program for Women, Infants, and Children (WIC)

❏ Free or Reduced Price School Lunch

Note: TANF may have a different name in your parents' state. Call 1-800-4-FED-AID to find out the name of the state's program.

Did your parents have any of the following items in 2015?

Check all that apply. Once online, you may be asked to report amounts paid or received by your parents.

Additional Financial Information	Untaxed Income	
❏ American Opportunity Tax Credit or Lifetime Learning Tax Credit	❏ Payments to tax-deferred pension and retirement savings plans	❏ Housing, food and other living allowances paid to members of the military, clergy and others
❏ Child support paid	❏ Child support received	
❏ Taxable earnings from work-study, assistantships or fellowships	❏ IRA deductions and payments to self-employed SEP, SIMPLE and Keogh	❏ Veterans noneducation benefits
❏ Taxable college grant and scholarship aid reported to the IRS	❏ Tax exempt interest income	❏ Other untaxed income not reported, such as workers' compensation or disability benefits
❏ Combat pay or special combat pay	❏ Untaxed portions of IRA distributions	
❏ Cooperative education program earnings	❏ Untaxed portions of pension distributions	

Your parents may be asked to provide more information about their assets.
Your parents may need to report the net worth of their current businesses and/or investment farms.

NOTES:

SECTION 4 - STUDENT INFORMATION

Did you know?

If you file a tax return with the IRS, you may be eligible to use the IRS Data Retrieval Tool, which is the easiest way to provide accurate tax information. With just a few simple steps, you may be able to view your tax return information and securely transfer it into *FAFSA on the Web*.

Did you file or will you file a 2015 income tax return?

❑ I have already completed my tax return

❑ I will file, but I have not completed my tax return

❑ I'm not going to file an income tax return

What was your (and spouse's) adjusted gross income for 2015?

Skip this question if you or your spouse did not file taxes. Adjusted gross income is on IRS Form 1040—Line 37; 1040A—line 21; or 1040EZ—line 4.

$ _____

The following questions ask about earnings (wages, salaries, tips, etc.) in 2015. Answer the questions whether or not a tax return was filed. This information may be on the W-2 forms, or on the IRS Form 1040—Line 7 + 12 +18 + Box 14 (Code A) of IRS Schedule K-1 (Form 1065); 1040A—line 7; or 1040EZ—line 1.

How much did you earn from working in 2015?

❑ Check here if you are a dislocated worker

$ _____

How much did your spouse earn from working in 2015?

❑ Check here if your spouse is a dislocated worker

$ _____

In 2014 or 2015, did anyone in your household receive: (Check all that apply.)

❑ Supplemental Security Income (SSI)   ❑ Temporary Assistance for Needy Families (TANF)

❑ Supplemental Nutrition Assistance Program (SNAP)   ❑ Special Supplemental Nutrition Program for Women, Infants, and Children (WIC)

❑ Free or Reduced Price School Lunch

Note: TANF may have a different name in your state. Call 1-800-4-FED-AID to find out the name of the state's program.

Did you or your spouse have any of the following items in 2015?

Check all that apply. Once online, you may be asked to report amounts paid or received.

Additional Financial Information

❑ American Opportunity Tax Credit or Lifetime Learning Tax Credit

❑ Child support paid

❑ Taxable earnings from work-study, assistantships or fellowships

❑ Taxable college grant and scholarship aid reported to the IRS

❑ Combat pay or special combat pay

❑ Cooperative education program earnings

Untaxed Income

❑ Payments to tax-deferred pension and retirement savings plans

❑ Child support received

❑ IRA deductions and payments to self-employed SEP, SIMPLE and Keogh

❑ Tax exempt interest income

❑ Untaxed portions of IRA distributions

❑ Untaxed portions of pension distributions

❑ Housing, food and other living allowances paid to members of the military, clergy and others

❑ Veterans noneducation benefits

❑ Other untaxed income not reported, such as workers' compensation or disability benefits

❑ Money received or paid on your behalf

You may be asked to provide more information about your (and your spouse's) assets.
You may need to report the net worth of current businesses and/or investment farms.

NOTES:

Do not mail this Worksheet. Go to www.fafsa.gov to complete and submit your application.

For more information on federal student aid, visit **StudentAid.gov**.
You can also talk with your college's financial aid office about other types of student aid that may be available.

Glossary

529 College Savings Plan (529 Plan): State-sponsored investments that allow families to save money for college expenses. The funds grow tax-free, and when withdrawn, the funds must be used for qualified educational expenses.

Academic Year: A period of time that usually consists of two semesters or three quarters.

Accrued Interest: Interest that accumulates on loans and must be paid at a later date.

Adjusted Gross Income (AGI): The income figure taken from the federal income tax form. AGI is the total of wages, interest, dividend, and other income minus certain adjustments.

Asset Protection Allowance: An allowance, subtracted from a family's total assets, used to determine the expected family income in need analysis. This allowance increases with age, recognizing that more assets should be available as you get closer to retirement age.

Assets: Financial holdings such as bank accounts, stocks, bonds and other securities, loan receivables, home and other real estate equity, business equipment, and business inventory.

Auto-Zero EFC: Low-income students who are eligible to file an IRS form 1040A or 1040EZ or who receive certain means-tested federal benefits will have their EFC automatically set to zero.

Award Letter: A college's notification of financial aid qualification. The award letter usually provides information about the types and amounts of aid offered, specific program information, and the conditions that govern the award.

Base Year: The twelve-month period ending on the December 31 that is used in the calculation of the EFC. The base year is the year two years prior to the award year. For example, 2015 is the base year for the 2017–18 award year.

Billing Servicer: A company that manages billing and loan collection for lenders and/or the federal government.

Business/Farm Supplement: A form required of parents and students who own a business or farm. This form is processed by the College Scholarship Service as a supplement to the Financial Aid PROFILE®.

Campus-Based Programs: The three federal financial aid programs administered by eligible colleges, including the Federal Supplemental Educational Opportunity Grant (FSEOG), Federal Work-Study (FWS), and Federal Perkins Loans.

Cancellation of Loan: A portion or all of some student loans can be canceled if the borrower performs service in certain geographic or academic fields. Some loans will be canceled upon the death of the borrower. Promissory notes describe the circumstances and conditions under which loans can be canceled.

Collection Agency: A company that specializes in collecting payment on default or delinquent loans. Collection agencies usually receive a percentage of the amount they collect from borrowers whose payments are overdue.

College Board: The nonprofit membership organization of colleges, secondary schools, and education associations. It administers the SAT, Financial Aid PROFILE®, and provides other education-related services.

Compound Interest: Interest that is computed on the sum of an original principal and any accrued interest.

Cooperative Education: A program offered by some colleges in which students alternate periods of enrollment with periods of employment, usually paid employment.

Cost of Attendance (Cost of Education): The costs associated with attending college for one academic year. Costs are determined by colleges themselves and usually include tuition and fees, room and board, books and supplies, transportation, and miscellaneous and personal expenses.

Credit Bureau: An agency that keeps credit histories and other information and reports this information to lenders.

Custodial Parent: The parent with whom the student lived the most during the twelve-month period prior to submitting the FAFSA. If the student lived equally with both parents, the custodial parent is the parent who provided more support during the twelve-month period prior to submitting the FAFSA.

Default: When a borrower fails to make payments on a loan for a specified period of time or has failed to comply with other terms of a promissory note.

Deferment: A specified period during which a borrower does not have to repay a loan. Depending on the type of loan, interest may or may not continue to accrue during a deferment period.

Dependency Override: Financial aid administrators may determine that a student is independent even if he or she does not meet the required eligibility criteria. A dependency override is done on a case-by-case basis and there must be documented unusual circumstances.

Dependent Student: An undergraduate student under the age of twenty-four who is not a veteran of the US Armed Forces, not married, not a ward of the court, and does not have legal dependents.

Delinquency: When a borrower fails to make an installment payment when it's due.

Direct Consolidation Loan: A federal loan made by the US Department of Education that allows you to combine one or more federal student loans into one new loan with one payment instead of multiple payments.

Direct Costs: Education-related expenses (tuition, fees, books, supplies) that a family generally pays to a college.

Disclosure Statement: A statement from a lender to a borrower that provides the borrower with information about the terms of the loan and the consequences of defaulting on that loan.

Discretionary Income: In the institutional methodology (IM) of need analysis, the income that is available to a family after taxes, medical expenses, and employment income protection and elementary/secondary tuition allowances have been subtracted. For income-based repayment plans, it is the difference between your income and loan-specific percentage of the poverty guideline for your family size and state of residence.

Eligible Noncitizen: A student aid applicant who is not a US citizen but is eligible to receive federal financial aid because he or she is a permanent resident, noncitizen national, or a resident of the Trust Territory of the Pacific Islands or Micronesia.

Enrollment Status: Either full-time, half-time, part-time, and so on, based on the number of credit hours in which a student is enrolled.

Entrance Interview: A required counseling session that may be online during which a college must inform student borrowers about their rights and responsibilities.

Exit Interview: Similar to an entrance interview, a counseling session that may be online and before the student borrower is leaving school. At the interview, a student's loan obligations and responsibilities are reviewed.

Expected Family Contribution (EFC): The figure that indicates how much of a family's financial resources should be available to help pay for educational expenses. The figure is calculated using a government-approved formula and determines eligibility for financial aid.

Federal Direct Loan: A family of federal student loan programs for which the lender is the federal government. See William D. Ford Federal Direct Loan (Direct Loan) Program. Included in these programs are the Direct Loans, Direct Unsubsidized Loans, Direct PLUS Loans, and Direct Consolidation Loans.

Federal Family Educational Loan Program (FFELP): A family of former federal student loans for which the lender is a bank, savings and loan, credit union, or other private lender. Included in these programs are government subsidized loans for students and unsubsidized loans for students and parents of undergraduate students. See Federal Stafford Loan.

Federal Methodology (FM): A need analysis formula developed by Congress and used to calculate the EFC, which determines eligibility for federal student aid programs.

Federal Pell Grant: A federal grant awarded to undergraduate students based on need as determined using a federal need analysis formula.

Federal Perkins Loan: A 5 percent loan awarded by colleges to both undergraduate and graduate students based on need as determined using a federal need analysis formula.

Federal Stafford Loan: A family of former federal student loans for which the lender is a bank, savings and loan, credit union, or other private lender. Included in these programs are government subsidized loans for students and unsubsidized loans for students and parents of undergraduate students.

Federal Student Aid Information Center (FSAIC): The customer service sponsored by the US Department of Education that answers questions about federal student aid and the FAFSA. The toll-free hotline number is 1-800-FED-AID (1-800-433-3243).

Federal Supplemental Educational Opportunity Grant (FSEOG): A federal grant awarded by colleges to the neediest undergraduates as determined by a federal need analysis formula.

Federal Work-Study (FWS): A federal need-based financial aid program through which eligible students earn a portion of their college expenses. Work-study is awarded by colleges, and a portion of the funding comes from the federal government. Several states also have work-study programs that are similar to the federal program.

Financial Aid Transcript: A form used by colleges to collect data about financial aid received at any previously attended college.

Financial Aid Award: A specific amount of financial assistance offered to a student through financial aid programs.

Financial Need: The difference between the cost to attend the college and the family's ability to pay, as measured by the EFC.

Forbearance: When a lender allows a borrower to temporarily stop paying a loan or agrees to accept smaller payments than previously scheduled. Usually forbearance is only given when personal problems such as short-term unemployment or hospitalization prevents a borrower from making loan payments.

Free Application for Federal Student Aid (FAFSA): The financial aid application all students must use to apply for federal student aid. The FAFSA is also used by many state agencies and colleges to award their own aid.

Full-Time: Usually when a student is enrolled in twelve or more semester or quarter hours per academic term.

Grace Period: The period of time that begins when a student loan borrower graduates or ceases to be enrolled at least half-time and ends when repayment must begin. The grace period for most student loans is six months.

Half-Time: Usually when a student is enrolled in six to eight semester or quarter hours per academic term.

Income-Driven Repayment Plan: A repayment schedule that allows borrowers to pay an amount based on their income. There are several student loan income-driven repayment plans that require borrowers to repay a portion of their discretionary income.

Independent Student: Any student who meets the following criteria: is at least twenty-four years old, is enrolled in a graduate or professional school, has legal dependents other than a spouse, is a ward or orphan of the court, is a veteran of the US Armed Forces, or is married.

Institutional Methodology: An alternate method of need analysis used by individual colleges to calculate the EFC used to determine eligibility for institutional and nonfederal aid.

Merit-Based Aid: Any form of financial aid awarded on the basis of personal achievement of individual characteristics and not based on demonstrated financial need.

Need Analysis Formula: A formula used to determine the amount a family is expected to contribute toward college expenses. This formula takes into account the family's financial strength and includes both income and assets.

Net Price: The difference between the full cost to attend the college and the gift aid the student receives.

Net Price Calculator: An online tool all colleges must have that provides a personalized estimate of what the net cost to attend will be based on information the student provides. It is an estimate, not an actual award, and is based on average awards at the college.

Overaward: A situation that occurs when a student's EFC plus any financial aid awarded exceeds the cost of attendance. Overawards result most often when a student's enrollment status changes or when additional resources become available to a student (such as an outside scholarship).

Prior-Prior Year: The base year for determining eligibility for federal student aid. It is the year *before* the prior tax year and a year and a half before enrollment. For example, the base year (prior-prior year) for enrollment in September 2017 is the 2015 tax year.

Professional Judgment: The law allows a financial aid administrator to change the calculated EFC or any of the elements used in the calculation based on additional information or individual circumstances that would lead to a more accurate assessment of the family's financial condition.

Promissory Note: The legal document that a borrower must sign when obtaining a loan. It lists the conditions under which the loan is made and the terms under which the borrower agrees to pay back the loan.

Repayment Schedule: A plan that sets forth the interest rate on a loan, the frequency of payments, the principal and interest due in each installment, the number of payments required to pay back the loan in full, and the due date of each payment.

Satisfactory Academic Progress: A term defined by each college that describes a satisfactory rate of course completion as well as individual term performance. Regulations require that a student make satisfactory progress toward a degree in order to receive federal aid.

Simplified Needs Test: A formula using the FM for those families whose AGI is less than $50,000 and who file either the 1040A or the 1040EZ IRS forms. When using this formula, the family's assets are not included.

Student Aid Report (SAR): An official document that can be electronic that colleges use to award federal aid. The SAR shows the calculated EFC as determined using the federal need analysis formula and based on information reported on the FAFSA.

Subsidized Loan: A loan for which the borrower is not responsible for interest while the student is enrolled in school at least half-time and during a grace period.

TEACH Grant: Although called a "grant," it is actually a forgivable loan that requires recipients to work as a teacher in a national need area for a specific number of years. If the recipient does not fulfill the service obligation, the "grant" converts to a loan.

Unmet Need: When a student's financial aid package (award) does not meet the calculated need (the difference between the cost of attendance and the EFC).

Verification: The process of substantiating data that a financial aid applicant reports on a financial aid application.

About the Author

Bart Astor

Bart Astor has more than thirty years of experience in higher education administration and student financial aid, serving as director of financial aid at several colleges and representing the National Association of State Student Grant and Aid Programs in Washington, DC. He is the author of twelve books, including the *Washington Post* bestseller *AARP Roadmap for the Rest of Your Life*, and was the publisher and founder of the *College Planning Quarterly*. Bart has a bachelor of arts from Carnegie Mellon University and a master's in public administration from San Jose State University.

Bart has appeared on numerous television and radio shows, including ABC's "Good Morning America," PBS's "MarketPlace," and Ric Edelman's "The Truth About Money."

He and his wife live in Reston, Virginia, with their two border collies, Bailey and Skye. You can follow Bart on Facebook (Bart Astor), Twitter (@bartastor), and his website, www.bartastor.com.

Index

Page numbers in italics refer to figures and tables.